Travis Barnes

BRAVE
in the making

A teen's guide
to taking back
their destiny
in God.

Brave In The Making
Copyright 2022 ©Travis Barnes

Published by Star Label Publishing
P.O. Box 1511, Buderim, QLD, Australia
publishing@starlabel.com.au
www.starlabelpublishing.com

Editing: Rebecca Moore and David Goodwin
Interior design: Rebecca Moore
Cover art: Tony Moore
Main image licensed 2022 Shutterstock

1st Edition April 2022

All rights reserved. No part of this publication may be reproduced in any form; stored in a retrieval system; or transmitted; or used in any other form; or by any other means without prior written permission of the publisher (except for brief quotes for the purpose of review or promotion).

Unless otherwise indicated, all Scripture quotations are taken from the Holy Bible, New Living Translation, copyright © 1996, 2004, 2007, 2013 by Tyndale House Foundation. Used by permission of Tyndale House Publishers, Inc., Carol Stream, Illinois 60188. All rights reserved

Scripture quotations marked (NIV) are taken from the Holy Bible, New International Version®, NIV®. Copyright © 1973, 1978, 1984, 2011 by Biblica, Inc.™ Used by permission of Zondervan. All rights reserved worldwide. www.zondervan.com. The "NIV" and "New international Version" are trademarks registered in the United States Patent and Trademark Office by Biblica, Inc.™

Scripture quotations marked (ISV) are taken from the Holy Bible: International Standard Version® Release 2.0. Copyright © 1996-2013 by the ISV Foundation. Used by permission of Davidson Press, LLC. ALL RIGHTS RESERVED INTERNATIONALLY.

Scripture quotations marked (ESV) are from The Holy Bible, English Standard Version® (ESV®), copyright © 2001 by Crossway, a publishing ministry of Good News Publishers. Used by permission. All rights reserved.

Scripture quotations marked (GNT) are from the Good News Translation in Today's English Version- Second Edition Copyright © 1992 by American Bible Society. Used by Permission.

The views expressed here-in remain the sole responsibility of the author, who exempts the publisher from all liability. The author and publisher do not assume responsibility for any loss, damage, or disruption caused by the contents, errors or omissions, whether such contents, errors, or omissions result from opinion, negligence, accident, or any other cause, and hereby disclaim any and all liability to any party.

ISBN: 978-0-6453697-0-0

ENDORSEMENTS

There are a great many obstacles faced by Christian young people seeking to understand what it means to live for Jesus today and into their futures. *Brave in the Making* lights a path for those who are serious about following Jesus, equipping them to seek God, to look to the Bible for guidance and ask the right questions on what it means to be brave followers of Jesus Christ in a world that is always changing and at times can seem hostile to their faith journeys. This is a great resource both for youth leaders looking for engaging discussion topics as well as for young people to work through on their own.

—**Neale Meredith**
Principal & Dean of Students
Australian College of Ministries

Travis writes with an eagerness to encourage and empower young people who desire to live bravely for the sake of the Kingdom. Capturing stories of great bravery, both modern and from the Bible, he highlights the courage needed to be a follower of Christ. A brilliant read, and highly recommended to all who are daring to be brave.

—**Bethany Francis**
Teacher
Pacific Hills Christian School

Brave in the Making is a God-inspired recount of the lives of some who live today and some who lived in Bible times. Travis has combined parts of each of their stories to encourage both young and old to be brave and reach for all God has prepared for them. As you read this book may you hear God speak to you, as I did, and know that 'Jesus—here He comes' for you.

—**Coral Maxwell**
Principal
Creek Street Christian College

Our students need to hear this message: In a generation being conditioned to be 'risk-minimisers' Barnes inspires us to be brave, to dream big to fulfill our God-designed potential. One of the greatest needs of our current generation is to not accept the lie that average is good enough. Barnes reminds us we serve a mighty God able to do more than we can possibly imagine. We need a new generation of leaders willing to be brave to achieve great things rather than accept a dumbed-down life. Schools, youth-groups and youth should use this book to redefine their culture and potential.

—**Jeremy Dover**
Teacher
Waverley Christian College

A riveting exploration of Christlike courage in all its fullness. *Brave in the Making* will ignite Godly passion in the next generation.

—Jay Johnstone
Teacher
Bayside Christian College

I love Travis' stories—they are true, sporty and spot on. And the Bible principles accompanying each story are so appropriate. Can't wait to see how students and their parents use the stories for their bedtime stories, devotions and Bible Studies! A wonderful resource for staff and for families.

—Phil Chapman
Former Principal
Olivet Christian College

Brave in the Making is a toolkit for energizing and equipping today's young people to follow Christ with confidence and courage. An action-packed read full of mind-boggling stories!

—**Rev. Dr. Mark Tronson**
Former Chaplain to the Australian Cricket Team

DEDICATION

To my King Jesus
You cast out all fear with your perfect love.
You must become greater; I must become less.

To my wife Cara
You continually pursue greater intimacy with the Father
and each year become braver and more joyful.

To my daughters Torah and Shiloh
You are bearers of a great message;
you host the presence of God.
You are brave in the making.

To all who have mentored and discipled me,
to all who have co-laboured in the gospel alongside me,
thanks for encouraging me to courageously pursue
Jesus.

Contents

Life on the Line	1
Date with Destiny	9
Fake It Till You Make It	17
A Giant Upset	25
Courage Under Fire	33
A Knockout Wedding	41
The Never-ending Match	49
Australia's Got Talent	57
Transformed by Trouble	63
A Blind Date	71
The Wife Carry	79
Drilling into Fear	87
Here He Comes	95
The Fast Lane	103

Miner Miracle	111
Noisy Pirates	117
Jail House Rock	125
Prison Break	133
Making a Splash	141
Dive for the Line	149
About the Author	157

x

1.

Life on the Line

Brave is taking risks

Day after day, Nik Wallenda puts his life on the line. Literally.

Wallenda is a tightrope walker who holds over ten Guinness World Records for his acrobatic feats, and has performed some of the most daring and dangerous tightrope walking attempts in history. In 2012, Wallenda became the first person to tightrope walk directly over Niagara Falls, and in 2013 walked across the Grand Canyon without a safety harness. Then, in 2020, Wallenda walked across the active Masaya Volcano.

My favourite of Wallenda's walks took place in 2014, when he walked between two skyscrapers to cross the Chicago River. He walked more than 600 feet above the ground with no safety harness and, as if that wasn't dangerous enough, the buildings were not the same height and Wallenda was forced to walk uphill on an incline of 19 degrees. And, after successfully completing that walk, he went on to perform a second one between two buildings—blindfolded!

A committed Christian who can be heard praying and thanking God as he walks, Nik Wallenda divides opinion. Some aren't sure whether he's brave, crazy-brave, or just crazy, but—like him or not—he's impossible to ignore. His skyscraper walk in Chicago was broadcast to television viewers in over 200 countries across the world and was Discovery Channel's most-watched live telecast for the year.

Can you imagine a world where people didn't take courageous risks? A world where people didn't live with an adventurous spirit? Imagine a world where Neil Armstrong hadn't walked on the moon and Edmund Hillary hadn't climbed Mount Everest. Or a world where the Wright brothers hadn't flown a plane and Christopher Columbus never sailed a boat. Bill Gates, the founder of Microsoft, Steve Jobs, the founder of Apple, and Mark Zuckerberg, the founder of Facebook, were all university dropouts, but just imagine what the world would be like if they completed their courses like everyone was expecting. Bill Gates would be a lawyer, Zuckerberg a psychologist, and Steve Jobs a professor of literature. There would be no iPad, no Microsoft Word, no Facebook, no Xbox, no Pixar movies, no Toy Story, no Buzz Lightyear—and no one would have ever found Nemo or Dory!

Imagine if Christians throughout the centuries didn't make sacrificial risks to advance the gospel. What if Billy Graham never held an evangelistic rally, or William

Booth hadn't started The Salvation Army? Imagine if William Tyndale hadn't risked his life to translate the Bible into English—or if the Apostle Paul had just stayed home!

If you thought tightrope walking between two buildings next to impossible, we can find an even more impossible situation in the book of 1 Samuel.

To set the scene:
Israel is in a battle against their arch-rivals the Philistines. The Israelites and the Philistines have been fierce enemies for generations, and, during the reign of Israel's King Saul, it was the Philistines who had the upper hand.

King Saul has 3,000 troops ready for battle, and in response, the Philistines muster 3,000 chariots, 6,000 charioteers, and as many warriors as 'the grains of sand on the seashore'.[1] When the Israelites see how badly outnumbered they are, they go missing, hiding wherever they can. King Saul is camped at Gilgal, and his men are trembling with fear. Saul waits for seven days, but offers no ideas, no leadership, and no hope. Saul is wasting time, waiting for someone else to be a hero. His forces rapidly shrink from 3000 to just 600. And, to make matters worse, the Israelites don't have any weapons! The Philistines are so dominant that they won't allow any blacksmiths to operate in the land of Israel, meaning that when an Israelite needs to sharpen their axe for cutting wood, or their sickle to cut grain, they are forced to pay a Philistine blacksmith.

---
[1] 1 Samuel 13:5

Having to pay a fee to their enemies is humiliating for the Israelites, and when it comes to the battle against the Philistines, only King Saul and his son Jonathan have swords. In one corner we have the Philistine army with troops numbering the grains of sand on the seashore, and in the other corner we have Israel with a vanishing army, no morale...and no weapons.

Jonathan's high wire act

It's against this gloomy backdrop that Jonathan steps up and takes action.

> "Come on," Jonathan says to his armour-bearer, "Let's go over to where the Philistines have their outpost."[2]

Jonathan is going rogue, and he doesn't tell his father, Saul, what he's planning. The idea that two men would take on an entire army is reckless and foolhardy. Like tightrope walking across Niagara Falls, Jonathan is asking for trouble. However, Jonathan is looking at this challenge from a different perspective. He's not making his decision based on the strength of Israel's army, but rather on the strength of God. Jonathan tells his armor-bearer:

> Perhaps the Lord will help us, for nothing can hinder the Lord. He can win a battle whether he has many warriors or only a few![3]

Jonathan would be remembering the story of Gideon, a previous judge of Israel who defeated the Midianite army which numbered many thousands with only three

---

[2] 1 Samuel 14:1.
[3] 1 Samuel 14:6

hundred troops. Jonathan knows something about God, he knows about God's power—which everyone else in Israel seems to have forgotten. Jonathan remembers that God doesn't need a big army to have a big victory. Jonathan isn't certain of victory, though. He says 'perhaps' the Lord will help us. Would you be willing to put your life on the line on the strength of a 'perhaps'?

When we take a step back and consider the big picture, the Israelites are in a bleak situation. Unarmed and outnumbered, they're on a hiding to nothing; they are cruising for a bruising. Jonathan might take a risk only to lose but, in all likelihood, they are going to lose anyway. Better to step out and take a risk with the possibility of 'perhaps' having a good outcome than hide in a cave and ensure defeat.

Jonathan is taking a courageous stand but he's mindful of God's leading as he does, he sets up a test[4] to ask for God's guidance. Jonathan plans to let the Philistines see them and, if the Philistines invite them to fight, Jonathan will take it as a sign that God will give them the victory. If the Philistines tell Jonathan to stay where they are, that will be Jonathan's sign not to engage in battle. When the Philistines see Jonathan, they shout "come on up here and we'll teach you a lesson!"[5] With that invitation Jonathan and his armour-bearer step forward.

Jonathan and his armour-bearer put their lives on the line, engaging the Philistines in battle and killing about

---

[4] This is similar to the time Gideon asks God to provide clarity on whether he should lead Israel by laying out a fleece. See Judges 6:36-40.
[5] 1 Samuel 14:12

twenty men. The Philistine army is suddenly struck with panic, and, on top of the confusion, God sends an earthquake, throwing the Philistines into total chaos.

One minute King Saul is losing troops, the next minute his troops are returning because the Philistines are in such disarray, they've begun fighting each other!

Israel has a great victory, all because Jonathan bravely stepped up when others stepped back. Importantly, Jonathan also had the support of his armour-bearer. His armour bearer didn't come up with this crazy plan, but he supported Jonathan's idea.

> "Do what you think is best," the armour-bearer replies, "I'm with you completely, whatever you decide."[6]

What would have happened if the armour-bearer was discouraging and said, "That'll never work"? Leaders need people who believe in them and will stand alongside them as they take daring risks. Sometimes we need to be like Jonathan and put forward the bold idea that's been stirring within us, and sometimes we need to be like the armour-bearer and support someone else who has a positive plan.

People, young and old, face many challenges. Some will sit around complaining about their problems saying that someone should do something about it. Some will give up, declaring the situation to be impossible.

"It'll never change," you'll hear the pessimists say,

---

[6] 1 Samuel 14:7

"They've tried and failed in the past, nothing ever changes."

Finally, you'll find some proactive leaders in the mould of Jonathan who ignore the talk, take the initiative, and, with God's help, bravely make change happen. It's often said those who say it cannot be done should not interrupt those who are doing it.

You can be a risk-taker like Jonathan when you remember that God is strong, and that God is with you. When you take a risk, step out and lead because, if you do, 'perhaps' there might be a good outcome. When you put yourself out there, risking failure because there are some things worth fighting for, you are brave in the making.

Bible Story: 1 Samuel 13-14

Press Pause: *Am I looking at my own strength and forgetting the strength of my God?*

Verse to remember:
For nothing is impossible with God. (Luke 1:37)

2.

Date with Destiny

Brave is speaking up

Eugene Bouchard is a Canadian tennis player. In 2014, she made the final of Wimbledon, reaching her career-best ranking of number five in the world. Bouchard is also prolific on social media with over a million followers online. One day, she wrote something on Twitter that she may have quickly wanted to take back.

February 5th, 2017 was a big day in American sport—the National Football League (NFL) Super Bowl. Over 100 million viewers tuned in to watch the Atlanta Falcons take on the New England Patriots. Atlanta dominated the game early leading 21-3 at halftime, and the game only deteriorated for the New England Patriots with Atlanta scoring in the third quarter to extend their lead to 28-3. At this point all the commentators agreed: the game was over, and it would take a miracle for the Patriots to come back and win.

Eugene Bouchard was watching the game and it was

at this point she decided to tell her one million twitter followers that, "I knew Atlanta would win." One of her followers named John Goehrke, a twenty-year-old student at the University of Missouri, decided it was time to declare his undying love for Eugene. He wrote back to the 22-year-old Bouchard saying, "If the Patriots win, we go on a date?" Bouchard was so confident of an Atlanta victory she replied with "Sure." It wasn't long after this that the Patriots scored a touchdown, the scoreboard now reading 28-9 heading into the final quarter.

Atlanta had dominated the game all day but, in the final quarter, the tide began to turn in the Patriot's favour. The Patriots did all the scoring in the final quarter but were still trailing the Falcons 28-20 with less than a minute to go. A last-minute touchdown levelled the scores at 28-28 as the final siren sounded, and the game was headed for extra time. Suddenly, Bouchard was starting to feel extremely nervous. She was now facing the very real prospect of having to go on a date with a total Twitter stranger. The New England Patriots scored in extra time to record the greatest comeback in Super Bowl history. As Captain Tom Brady held the Vince Lombardi Trophy aloft, Bouchard was on Twitter arranging a date, tweeting, "So where do you live?"

Bouchard was true to her word and she and Goehrke went to a basketball game together. The two of them got on so well they went on more dates including attending the following year's Super Bowl, and this time Bouchard wasn't making any predictions. It was an unlikely comeback and an unlikely date—Bouchard is a tennis superstar with a million twitter followers, while John

Date with Destiny

Goehrke is just an ordinary guy who found himself in the right place at the right time and took a risk which changed his life in the course of one dramatic quarter of football. When John Goehrke spoke up on Twitter, it changed his life, but in the Bible, we meet Esther who spoke up and saved a nation.

To set the scene:
Esther is an ordinary Jewish girl whose life is turned upside down by events beyond her control. She lives with her cousin Mordecai because her parents have died, but we have no details about this tragic event and the impact it had on her. Mordecai and Esther live in Susa, the capital of the Persian Empire which covers 127 provinces stretching from India to Ethiopia. They are Jews living far from their homeland because of another tumultuous event: The Babylonian invasion. Many decades earlier the Babylonian army invaded Jerusalem, taking Mordecai's family to a foreign land[7], and in time the Babylonian empire was conquered by a new power, the Persian Empire.

The King of the Persian Empire is called Xerxes and in the third year of his reign he throws a spectacular banquet lasting 180 days. Xerxes pulls out all the stops, no expense is spared as he shows off the great wealth and splendour of the Persian Empire. If 180 days of partying weren't enough, when it's all over the king throws another banquet lasting seven days for those in the fortress of Susa. The wine flows freely at this event and the king has an open bar policy. Everyone can drink as much as they like, and Xerxes is in high spirits because of the wine. The

---

[7] Esther 2:6

King gets a little tipsy, singing out of tune karaoke and falling off his barstool, before summoning the Queen to show her off to everyone. Ordering his servants to bring out Queen Vashti so that everyone can gaze at her beauty, Xerxes is treating Vashti as a trophy wife, wanting to show her off to boost his ego.

Queen Vashti, understandably but perhaps unwisely, turns down the King's demands. We begin to learn what happens in Persia when you displease the King when Vashti is deposed as Queen, never to be seen again. The King wakes up the next day with a splitting headache and realises he doesn't have a queen anymore, which makes him sad because he quite liked Vashti. To cheer him up, his servants propose searching the Kingdom to find beautiful young women, with the woman who most pleases the King becoming queen in Vashti's place. Let's be clear, the king isn't looking for a wife. He's looking for a supermodel—less of a wife and more of a reality show contest winner. The King likes Esther far more than any of the other contestants and makes her the queen. In our day, we have the freedom to marry or to not marry—Esther has no choice. She could refuse, but, like Vashti, if she does, she will never be seen again.

Overnight, she goes from obscurity, to becoming the Queen of Persia, but Esther has a secret. She's Jewish, but Mordecai advises Esther never to tell anyone about her nationality for own her safety. There are people in high places with agendas against the Jewish people, and one of these people is Haman—the most prominent official in all Persia. He is an Agagite, a people that had been

Date with Destiny

defeated generations earlier by Israel's King Saul.[8]

Haman is a power-hungry, self-obsessed, showboating megalomaniac[9], and when Mordecai refuses to tickle Haman's ego by bowing to him, Haman is enraged. And it's not enough for Haman to remove one Jew, he must remove them all! Haman uses deception and bribery to convince Xerxes to destroy the Jewish people. The news travels around the kingdom of the Jews' impending doom, yet Haman doesn't know that the Queen herself is Jewish.

Mordecai sends a message to Esther alerting her to the plight of the Jews, but Esther's reply is underwhelming. She reminds Mordecai that you can't simply waltz into the king's office and help yourself to his fridge. You can only see the King when he invites you, go uninvited and you might never be seen again. Esther adds that she's not very influential around the palace anyway, she hasn't seen the King in over 30 days.

Mordecai tells Esther two things in response, firstly: that God will rescue the Jewish people with or without her and, second: that perhaps that God made her queen for this very moment. Esther is in the right place at the right time—will she take a risk to save her family and her people?

Esther tells Mordecai to ask everyone to pray, and three days later she puts on her royal robes and enters the inner court. She doesn't know if the King will welcome her or if it will be the end of her.

---

[8] You can read about this in 1 Samuel 15.
[9] He's very self-important

Queen Esther's date with destiny

The King holds out his royal sceptre to welcome Esther, asking her, "What do you want, Queen Esther? What is your request?"[10]

Esther invites the King and Haman to dinner—and we know how much the King enjoys a feast! At the banquet, the King is eager to know what Esther's request is, but Esther still won't divulge her secret. She asks the King to come to a second banquet where she will finally reveal her secret—it will be her date with destiny.

It takes three opportunities, but Esther finally spills the beans. She bravely reveals her identity to the King and tells the King about Haman's plot to annihilate the Jewish people, who becomes faint as his evil plan is exposed. Haman is deposed and never seen again, Mordecai is promoted to replace Haman, and Esther and Mordecai issue a new law to save the Jewish people.

There are times in life when it's important to speak up and speak out against what is wrong. It won't be easy; speaking out can be risky with plenty of downsides. You might be tempted to keep quiet as Esther was, but God helped Esther overcome her fears, and He can help you overcome yours. When you speak up for what's right, you are brave in the making.

---

10   Esther 5:3

Date with Destiny

Bible Story: This story is found in the Book of Esther.

Press Pause: *Is there something I need to speak up about?*

Verse to remember:
Don't be afraid, because I'm with you. Don't be anxious because I am your God. (Isaiah 41:10 ISV)

3.

Fake It Till You Make It

Brave is trusting God despite your feelings

Elizabeth Swaney had a dream of becoming a winter Olympian. After attempting bobsled, skeleton, and aerial skiing without success, she decided to make her mark in the sport of half-pipe skiing. This involves skiing while performing tricks such as flips, spins, and grabs. Sadly, for Elizabeth Swaney, she couldn't do any of these.

There was little chance she would be selected to compete in half-pipe skiing for the country where she was born. The United States has 325 million people, most of who were better at half-pipe skiing than she was. So, Swaney decided to compete for the nation of Hungary, her grandparents' country of birth. Hungary has just under

10 million people, giving her a better chance of Olympic selection.

The question remained—how was Elizabeth Swaney going to qualify for Olympic half-pipe skiing when she couldn't even do the sport?

There were two criteria for Olympic selection:

- The world's top 24 skiers will be selected but only a maximum of four from any one nation.
- Athletes must place in the top 30 in a recognized halfpipe competition.

These looked like difficult criteria to meet given Swaney's lack of ability. However, she was undeterred and decided to enter a half pipe competition. Swaney travelled to New Zealand, entered a competition, and came in 26th place. How did she pull off such a feat when she couldn't even perform the simplest of tricks? Swaney started at one end, skied to the other, performed no tricks and came in last place. But importantly, there were only 26 athletes in the competition. This fulfilled one of the two criteria, she had finished in the top 30 in a recognized halfpipe competition.

But how would Swaney get her ranking up to be one of the twenty-four athletes at the Olympic Games? When Swaney finished 26th in New Zealand she earnt herself some ranking points—not many, but it was a start. Swaney figured that, if she needed more points, she simply needed to enter more competitions. So Swaney went to Canada and came 21st, to South Korea and came 26th, France 24th, and Spain 21st. In China she finished 13th—how did she manage that? There were only 15 competitors and two of them crashed out. Swaney also competed all around America, accruing points and improving her ranking. As the Olympics drew near, Swaney found herself ranked 34th in the world. Consider Elizabeth Swaney's monumental achievement—she was ranked 34th in the world for a sport she didn't even do!

Swaney's world ranking was close but just shy of Olympic selection. Then, some technicalities began to run in her favour. America had six skiers in the top 24 but was only allowed to send their best four. Swaney avoided that by competing for Hungary. Some of the world's top 24 were injured—half-pipe skiing is a dangerous sport, especially for those who perform tricks. As a result, the Olympic Committee kept going further and further down the list. Eventually, they found themselves inviting Hungary's Elizabeth Swaney to the Olympic Games. Elizabeth, take a bow!

What a remarkable achievement! Elizabeth Swaney went to the 2018 winter games in a sport she couldn't do for a country she didn't live in. On the day of her event, she started at one end, skied to the other, performed no tricks, and finished in last place. There were 2,922 athletes at the 2018 winter games and Swaney was surely the most unlikely of them all.

If you thought Elizabeth Swaney making the Olympics was unlikely, we're about to encounter one of the most unlikely leaders in the Bible. His name is Gideon, and we meet this brave warrior hiding in a hole.

To set the scene:
Gideon belongs to the nation of Israel, which at this time is being severely persecuted by the nation of Midian. The Midianites attack Israel's farms, destroying their crops and reducing Israel to starvation. This happens at a time when Israel isn't following the Lord. The Angel of the Lord appears to Gideon who is threshing wheat in a winepress. You don't need to be an expert to know that winepresses are for pressing grapes to make wine, not for threshing wheat, but Gideon has chosen this unconventional location to hide from the Midianites.

The Angel of the Lord speaks to Gideon and says, "Mighty hero, the Lord is with you!"

Has there been a mistake? Did the Angel go to the wrong hole? Israel's hopes of freedom rest on the shoulders of a hero in hiding.

Gideon replies, "If the Lord is with us why has all this happened to us?"

Gideon doesn't get it; he doesn't even realise that Israel is suffering because of their disobedience.[11]

Gideon offers excuses: "How can I rescue Israel? My clan is the weakest in the whole tribe of Manasseh, and I am the least in my entire family!"

But the fact that Gideon is weak is exactly the reason God uses him. God wants to show Israel that it is God who will rescue them from the Midianites, not a strong warrior.

---

[11] Judges 6:1 The Israelites did evil in the Lord's sight. So, the Lord handed them over to the Midianites for seven years.

The Lord offers Gideon further encouragement: "I will be with you. And you will destroy the Midianites as if you were fighting against one man."

Gideon asks if he can bring God a voluntary offering. This is a great move, as a voluntary offering is a way to worship God. Gideon may be weak, but he offers God what he has. God accepts Gideon's offering; the Angel of the Lord touches the gift with the tip of his staff and fire consumes it and the Angel disappears! A miraculous event—this should give Gideon the encouragement he needs to be brave…

Next, God tells Gideon to pull down his father's altar to Baal, which is an idol that Israel worships instead of God. Gideon plucks up the courage to pull the idol down, but at night when no one's watching. It's braver than hiding in a hole—but not by much.

Now Gideon asks God to prove to him that He plans to use him. If Gideon wants a sign all he needs to do is open his eyes! The Angel of the Lord has appeared to him and personally told him he would rescue Israel. Plus, Gideon's offering was consumed by fire. But God is remarkably patient with Gideon's questioning. When Gideon puts out a woollen fleece and asks God to make the fleece wet and the ground dry, God grants his request.

Gideon then says to God:

> Please don't be angry with me, let me make one more request. Let me use the fleece for one more test. This time let the fleece remain dry while the ground around it is

wet with dew.[12]

God is gracious, He knows how scared Gideon is. The next morning the fleece is dry, and the ground is wet. Finally, Gideon is convinced God is calling him to lead. He's not feeling it, but he gets on with it.

With a leader as weak as Gideon, you would think God would provide him with a strong army to give him confidence. Instead, God tells Gideon he has too many troops! The Midianite army has over 100,000 soldiers, Gideon has just 32,000. God is teaching the nation of Israel an important lesson. If God's people follow Him, He is more than able to protect them and win their battles. He can use the weakest leader with the smallest army to defeat the most powerful armies in the world. God tells Gideon's army that if anyone is scared, they can leave. 22,000 of Israel's soldiers breathe a sigh of relief and return home, leaving Gideon with just 10,000 troops. They are outnumbered by more than 10 to 1! But God decides it is necessary to reduce the army further, right down to just 300 men! Let's check out their weapons…

Gideon's troops are handed a ram's horn, which was a musical instrument. This army looks more like a brass band than it does a military force. Each man also has a clay pot with a torch inside (not a torch with batteries but more like a stick with a flame). These are not the sort of weapons you'd expect. Just after midnight Gideon's men blow their ram's horns and break their clay jars. One minute the Midianites are sleeping, the next minute there's sound and light everywhere. The Midianites panic

---
[12] Judges 6:39

and begin fighting one another and Israel wins an incredible victory in the most unlikely of circumstances.

If Elizabeth Swaney is the most improbable Olympian, then Gideon is the unlikeliest of leaders. Gideon's story reminds us, if God can use a man hiding in a hole to free His nation, then anyone can be brave in the making, even you!

Bible Story: Judges 6-7

Press Pause: *Am I underestimating what God can do through me?*

Verse to remember:
God chose what is foolish in the world to shame the wise, God chose what is weak in the world to shame the strong. (1 Corinthians 1:27 ESV)

4.

A Giant Upset

Brave is remembering who's with you

Steven Bradbury was a short track speed skater attending his fourth Olympic Games in Salt Lake City. In his first Olympics, he had been a backup member of the team and didn't skate, while in his second Olympics Bradbury was in the relay team and took home a bronze medal—Australia's first-ever medal at the Winter Olympics. Bradbury was often considered a medal contender in the individual events, the 500 metres and 1000 metres short track. But luck was not on Bradbury's side as collisions prevented him from reaching the finals in these events.

He also had rotten luck with injuries throughout his career. In 1994, he needed 111 stitches and lost four litres of blood after a terrible collision, while in 2000 he broke his neck in a training accident. Doctors told Bradbury his skating days were over, but Bradbury desperately wanted one more crack at the Olympics even though he realized he was now past his best.

Bradbury defied the odds and made it to his fourth Olympic Games at Salt Lake City in 2002. He was the second oldest competitor in the 1000 metre short track speed skate and didn't have the speed to match his competitors. He won his first heat, advancing to the quarterfinals and, in the quarterfinals, needed a top-two finish to advance to the semi-finals. But he faced stiff opposition. In the quarter-final he was up against American local hope Apolo Ohno, as well as defending world champion Canada's Marc Gagnon. Onho and Gagnon finished in first and second leaving Bradbury in third place and missing out on a place in the semi-final. Gagnon, however, was disqualified and Bradbury's Olympic quest was still alive. Then, in the semi-final, Bradbury was coming dead last when three of his competitors crashed—Bradbury had booked himself a spot in the Olympic final.

All the luck that eluded Bradbury during previous Olympics was suddenly coming his way. In the final, Bradbury was in last place from the beginning of the race. On the final lap, Apolo Ohno narrowly led three skaters with Bradbury 15 metres off the pace. As the pack jostled for the lead around the final bend they collided, all four competitors crashing into the wall. It was a total wipeout! Steven Bradbury was the last man standing, and he crossed the line for the Gold medal.

Bradbury said after the race, "Obviously I wasn't the fastest skater. I don't think I'll take the medal for the minute-and-a-half of the race I actually won. I'll take it for the last decade of the hard slog I put in."

Bradbury's win may have been the greatest ever Olympic

A Giant Upset

upset, but the Bible records another upset of giant proportions.

To set the scene:
The Philistines and the Israelites are sworn enemies who have fought each other for generations. The Philistines are on one hill and the Israelites are on the other when the Philistines wheel out their strongest warrior, Goliath. He is nine feet tall and would be an asset in any basketball team. Goliath taunts the Israelites:

> "Why are you all coming out to fight?" he calls. "I am the Philistine champion, but you are only the servants of Saul. Choose one man to come down here and fight me! If he kills me, then we will be your slaves. But if I kill him, you will be our slaves! I defy the armies of Israel today! Send me a man who will fight me!"[13]

King Saul should have fought Goliath. The Bible says that Saul is head and shoulders taller than anyone else in Israel,[14] and he's also the King of his nation when Israel is in need of a leader. Israel needs someone to remind them that the God of Israel is mightier than all the armies of the world. But Saul is shaking in his boots, deeply afraid. Saul has forgotten that God once defeated 100,000 Midianite soldiers with just 300 men under Gideon's leadership.

Instead of fighting, King Saul instead decides to offer a huge reward to the man who kills Goliath. The king promises his daughter in marriage to the successful man, and his entire family will be exempt from taxes. Saul is trying to bribe the men of Israel into doing what he isn't

---

13   1 Samuel 17:8-10
14   1 Samuel 9:2

brave enough to do himself.

For forty days the same routine occurs. Goliath taunts Israel, their army, and God, and the Israelites are too timid to respond to Goliath's challenge. David isn't part of the army since he's only a boy; his dad has just sent him to the battlefront to deliver food. As David is talking with his brothers, Goliath comes out to perform his usual routine of mocking the Israelites, and David is aghast at what he hears from Goliath.

David asks:

> Who is this pagan Philistine anyway, that he is allowed to defy the armies of the living God?[15]

David's oldest brother, Eliab, doesn't like the sound of David's enthusiasm. He scolds David:

> "What are you doing around here anyway?" he demands. "What about those few sheep you're supposed to be taking care of? I know about your pride and deceit. You just want to see the battle!"[16]

But, if David was there to see the battle, it isn't much of a spectacle. Eliab and his brave warriors hadn't mustered up the courage to do any fighting. Word filters back to King Saul that David is willing to fight Goliath and the king, desperate for a volunteer, calls for him. But, when he sees David, he dismisses the idea.

> "Don't be ridiculous!" Saul replied. "There's no way you

---

[15] 1 Samuel 17:26
[16] 1 Samuel 17:28

A Giant Upset

can fight this Philistine and possibly win! You're only a boy, and he's been a man of war since his youth."[17]

But David doesn't take no for an answer. He might be lacking in age and experience, but he possesses more than enough courage.

David tells Saul:

> When a lion or a bear comes to steal a lamb from the flock, I go after it with a club and rescue the lamb from its mouth. If the animal turns on me, I catch it by the jaw and club it to death. I have done this to both lions and bears, and I'll do it to this pagan Philistine, too, for he has defied the armies of the living God![18]

Saul isn't convinced. But he can't put off the battle with Goliath forever, so he allows David to fight. King Saul offers his armour, but a young man wearing the armour of the tallest man in Israel is not a good fit. Instead, David goes to a creek and picks up five smooth stones and, armed with only a sling and a shepherd's staff, he goes to face Goliath. Consider the odds of this matchup: in one corner, the nine-foot-tall Philistine warrior, Goliath, armed with a bronze helmet, armour, and javelin; in the other, David, a boy with a few pebbles. Goliath seems half-amused, half-insulted by David's challenge.

> "Am I a dog," he roars at David, "that you come at me with a stick?" And he cursed David by the names of his gods. "Come over here, and I'll give your flesh to the birds and wild animals!" Goliath yells.[19]

17	1 Samuel 17:33
18	1 Samuel 17:34-36
19	1 Samuel 17:43-44

David has one thing going in his favour—he remembers that God is mightier than Goliath. It seems that everyone in Israel has forgotten about the might and power of their God. David isn't confident in his own strength but has confidence in God's.

David speaks to the giant:

> You come to me with sword, spear, and javelin, but I come to you in the name of the Lord of Heaven's Armies—the God of the armies of Israel, whom you have defied. Today the Lord will conquer you, and I will kill you and cut off your head. And then I will give the dead bodies of your men to the birds and wild animals, and the whole world will know that there is a God in Israel! And everyone assembled here will know that the Lord rescues his people, but not with sword and spear. This is the Lord's battle, and he will give you to us![20]

Goliath moves to attack, but David runs toward him and hurls a stone with his sling. It travels through the air, hitting Goliath in the forehead, who falls to the ground. David doesn't have a sword, so he uses Goliath's sword to cut off its owner's head. Seeing their champion is dead, the Philistines make a run for it.

Perhaps you feel like David sometimes. Perhaps people look down on you, ignore you, or don't believe in you. But God notices you and you are important to him. You too will face big battles when you will feel outnumbered and overpowered, but when you face major obstacles and giant-sized challenges you need to remember that God is strong—and that God is with you. Remember that

---
[20] 1 Samuel 17:45-47

A Giant Upset

and you'll be ready to pull off a giant upset.

Bible Story: 1 Samuel 17

Press Pause: *Do I believe that God is with me as I face giants in my own life?*

Verse to remember:
If God is for us, who can be against us? (Romans 8:31 NIV)

5.

Courage Under Fire

Brave is saying no

In the state of Western Australia there is a peculiar area called Hutt River. The area contains five farms and about 30 people. The farms themselves aren't unusual; they produce wheat, grow wool, and raise lambs.

In 1970, Leonard Casey, a farmer from Hutt River, was embroiled in an argument with the Western Australian government over how much tax he had to pay. Who likes paying tax? Not Leonard Casey! He complained about it and wrote several angry letters, but nothing changed. So, one day Casey did something drastic—he declared that the area of Hutt River was no longer part of Australia! According to Casey, Hutt River was now its very own country called the Hutt River Province. Casey declared himself 'His Royal Highness, Prince Leonard', and even made a statue of himself in his honour.

Since Hutt River was now its own country, Prince Leonard argued they shouldn't have to pay Australian taxes. But, before you start turning your backyard into a new nation, understand that it doesn't work that way. Australia never recognized Hutt River as a separate country and the courts have found their arguments to be gobbledygook, with the Hutt River Province ending up owing millions of dollars in unpaid taxes. The Hutt River Province has its own flag, stamps, and number plates. They even have their own currency—conveniently, one Hutt River dollar is equal to one Australian dollar. If you took an international trip to the Hutt River Province, you'd find it's just a collection of farms with a cool gift shop.

At one point in 1977, Australia Post decided not to deliver the mail to Hutt River anymore, since they weren't really part of Australia. Prince Leonard was furious, sending a royal edict to the Governor-General of Australia on December 2nd, 1977, declaring war on Australia! The war raged on for several days, there was no sign of gunfire and no casualties to speak of, but the war was a great victory for the little nation of Hutt River because they got their mail back!

Prince Leonard died in 2019, but, before his death, he passed the throne to his son Graeme. Prince Graeme held several portfolios, serving as the foreign minister, minister for education, minister for finance, the minister responsible for the royal mint of Hutt River, and the Chancellor of the Hutt River Province Royal College of Advanced Research. All that work must have taken its toll on Prince Graeme, and so, in 2020, the decision was made to dissolve the nation of Hutt River and once again return to being part of the Commonwealth of Australia. Welcome back, Hutt River.

In the Bible, we find a King who thought very highly of himself, and like Prince Leonard, built a huge statue of himself.

To set the scene:
King Nebuchadnezzar conquers God's people in Judah and destroys its capital Jerusalem. Thousands of Jews are taken by force to the nation of Babylon to serve King Nebuchadnezzar, and he becomes the most powerful king in the world.

Nebuchadnezzar makes a gold statue, 90 feet high (or 10 Goliaths tall!). Earlier, Nebuchadnezzar had a dream of a huge statue. This statue's head was made of gold, its chest and arms were made from silver, its belly and thighs were made of bronze, its legs were iron, and its feet were part iron and part clay. Daniel interprets Nebuchadnezzar's dream, telling him that he is the head of gold but after him will come a kingdom inferior to his, hence the silver, then another inferior kingdom, made of bronze, and so on. Daniel says, in time the great kingdom of Babylon will come crashing down but God will set up a kingdom that lasts forever. The message is clear, Nebuchadnezzar's kingdom is temporary, God's kingdom is eternal.

No sooner do we turn the page, we find King Nebuchadnezzar is building himself a giant statue, but this statue is all gold. Nebuchadnezzar is defying God, saying his kingdom is made of gold and always will be. He's proclaiming to the world that his kingdom is eternal.

To make matters worse Nebuchadnezzar commands all the officials in his kingdom to worship the statue:

> When you hear the sound of the horn, flute, zither, lyre, harp, pipes, and other musical instruments, bow to the ground to worship King Nebuchadnezzar's gold statue. Anyone who refuses to obey will immediately be thrown into a blazing furnace.[21]

That's quite a musical ensemble Nebuchadnezzar has put together and there's every reason to obey—there's a fiery furnace waiting for anyone who might object.

There are three Jews who have responsibility for the province of Babylon: Shadrach, Meshach, and Abednego. They worship the true God and believe that He alone is worthy of worship. Shadrach, Meshach, and Abednego are caught between a rock and a hard place, they can't worship the statue as it would be an insult to their creator but, if they don't, they'll quite literally be fired. It's a life-or-death decision, but they refuse to worship the statue. Word filters back to Nebuchadnezzar and Shadrach, Meshach, and Abednego find themselves standing before the King. He decides to give them one more chance to worship or else they will be thrown into the fiery furnace. Shadrach, Meshach, and Abednego refuse to crack under pressure. They tell the king:

> O Nebuchadnezzar, we do not need to defend ourselves before you. If we are thrown into the blazing furnace, the God whom we serve is able to save us. He will rescue us from your power, Your Majesty. But even if he doesn't, we want to make it clear to you, Your Majesty, that we

---

[21] Daniel 3:5-6

will never serve your gods or worship the gold statue you have set up.[22]

These three Jews are not disrespectful towards the King, but they inform him that his authority has limits. He might be the King, but he is not God. They know God has the power to rescue them, but they're not certain if He will. Either way, their minds are made up, there's no turning back. They tell the king, "No."

Nebuchadnezzar flies into a rage, he isn't used to people telling him no. He orders the fire to be heated seven times hotter than normal. The fire doesn't kill the three Jews, but it does kill the soldiers as they throw Shadrach, Meshach, and Abednego into the flames.

Suddenly, Nebuchadnezzar jumps up in amazement and asks,

> Didn't we tie up three men and throw them into the furnace?[23]

> I see four men, unbound, walking around in the fire unharmed! And the fourth looks like a god.[24]

Nebuchadnezzar orders Shadrach, Meshach, and Abednego to come out of the fire. They're not harmed, they're not burnt, they don't even smell of smoke. Nebuchadnezzar has reached the limits of his authority, he attempted to kill these three men, but God overruled him. People have debated who exactly it was that was walking around in the fire with Shadrach, Meshach, and

---
22 Daniel 3:16-18
23 Daniel 3:24
24 Daniel 3:25

Abednego. Was it an angel? Was it Jesus himself? Whoever it was, what is clear is that God was in the fire with them. Nebuchadnezzar is humbled:

> Praise to the God of Shadrach, Meshach, and Abednego! He sent his angel to rescue his servants who trusted in him. They defied the king's command and were willing to die rather than serve or worship any god except their own God.[25]

The King promotes these brave men to higher positions in the kingdom. They risked their lives by saying no and now find themselves better off than before.

King Nebuchadnezzar thought he was bigger than God. He thought he could do whatever he wanted. Nebuchadnezzar was wrong. You too might be tempted to think you don't need God, that you don't need to listen to what He has to say about living. You might think that you can be like the Hutt River Province and run your own little kingdom in your own little way. But, as Nebuchadnezzar discovered, it doesn't work. We are not bigger than God. He made us. Our plans are temporary, His plans are forever.

God is with you when you need to be brave. When you need to speak up or stand up for what's right. When you need to stand your ground and say no. God stands with you even if you're standing alone.

---

[25] Daniel 3:28

Courage Under Fire

Bible Story: Daniel 3

Press Pause: *Who is pressuring me to do wrong? Who do I need to say no to?*

Verse to remember:
> When you pass through deep waters, I will be with you; your troubles will not overwhelm you. When you pass through fire, you will not be burned; the hard trials that come will not hurt you. (Isaiah 43:2 GNT)

6.

A Knockout Wedding

Brave is going back

Michael Reeves played 63 games of AFL football in the 1980s. In 1986, something special happened in Reeves' life; he became engaged to his partner, Kim. Michael and Kim wanted to have their wedding at a popular wedding venue, Montsalvat, in Melbourne's outer suburbs. Montsalvat was so popular there was only one date available, preliminary final day. Michael ruled it out as a possibility: AFL finals and weddings don't mix.

Michael was playing for the Fitzroy Lions (now known as the Brisbane Lions), who were struggling that year and needed a string of victories and a small miracle just to make the finals. The preliminary final, which is just one match before the AFL Grand Final, seemed out of reach. Reeves decided he would run the idea of booking his wedding by his coach.

The coach looked at Michael and said, "Mate, we're not

travelling too well at the moment, we need to win four out of the last five just to get to the finals, I think you're pretty safe, go and book it."

With the coach's blessing, Michael Reeves booked his wedding day for the same day as the preliminary final. What could possibly go wrong?

With five rounds left in the season, Fitzroy faced the Richmond Tigers. The Lions trailed for the first three quarters but put in a superb final quarter to run over the top of the Tigers and win by 11 points. Next up Fitzroy faced the bottom-placed Saint Kilda Saints. The Saints had won just two games all season and Fitzroy belted them to the tune of 85 points. The Lions lost their next match, but still had a chance at the finals if they won their last two games of the season. It was a tall order, their next match was against the defending champions, Essendon. Fitzroy kicked six goals in the opening quarter and ran away with a surprising 35-point victory. The Fitzroy Lions were now just one win away from a finals berth.

Fitzroy's last match of the season was against the second-placed Sydney Swans. It was a tight tussle, but the Lions held on for a 10-point win! The Fitzroy Lions had won four out of their last five games to scrape into the finals. Michael Reeves didn't need to worry just yet, though, the Lions still needed to win two matches before the preliminary final came around. The first final was called the elimination final—the winner lives on; the loser is eliminated. Once again, they were playing defending champions, the Essendon Bombers. The match was an arm-wrestle all day, and at three-quarter time the Bombers led by three points. The game went down to the wire, the

A Knockout Wedding

Lions won the match by a single point!

The Lions had advanced to the semis: a win here would book a spot in the preliminary final. The Lions faced the Swans whom they had beaten a fortnight previously, and at three-quarter time the Swans led by two goals. The Lions charged home, kicking five last quarter goals to win the match by five points. Suddenly, Michael Reeves had a very busy Saturday coming up!

The Preliminary Final between the Hawthorn Hawks and the Fitzroy Lions was set to be played on Saturday at 2:30 pm, while Michael and Kim were getting married at Montsalvat at 6 pm. How would Michael be able to play the game and make it to the wedding on time? Channel 7 came to Michael's rescue, offering him a helicopter ride to the wedding after the match. All Michael had to do was put on his boots, play some footy, win the game, hop in the chopper, put on a suit, walk down the aisle, and say, "I do". Easy as can be.

In the opening minutes, Michael Reeves ran onto the ground, collided with an opponent, and was knocked out. Reeves was carried off on a stretcher as the Fitzroy Lions were belted by 56 points—it wasn't the Saturday he'd been expecting! By the end of the game, Reeves had recovered just enough to walk to the chopper and fly to his wedding. Sometimes he tells his wife, "I don't remember marrying you!"

Michael Reeves' wedding didn't exactly go according to plan. Likewise, Moses is a leader in the Bible whose life took plenty of unexpected twists and turns.

To set the scene:
Moses, an Israelite, was born in Egypt during a time when the Israelites are suffering severe oppression by the nation of Egypt, and are enslaved and treated brutally. Such is the wickedness of the King of Egypt he orders that Israel's baby boys be thrown into the Nile River. The King of Egypt is a monster. An Israelite woman named Jochebed has a son and refuses to have him thrown in the river. When she can't hide him any longer, she makes a basket and places the baby inside, on the Nile River. Some movies capture this moment with Moses being swept along by the waves and rapids, dodging past hippos and crocodiles, but the Bible says she placed him in the reeds along the bank of the Nile—hardly a rushing torrent. Why did Jochebed place him there? Did she know who would come to bathe?

Pharaoh's daughter comes to the Nile to bathe and sees the little floating boat. She opens the basket and looks at the baby who looks back at the Princess and starts crying—he was hoping to see his mummy. This Princess isn't like her father at all, she has a heart of compassion and wants to adopt him. Right on cue, Moses' big sister Miriam jumps out from her hiding place and offers to get an Israelite midwife, and when the Princess agrees, Miriam runs and gets Jochebed.

"Take this baby and nurse him for me, and I will pay you,"[26] says the Princess.

What a change! Moses was facing execution, now he's been granted royal protection, while Jochebed is now

---

26   Exodus 2:8

A Knockout Wedding

being paid to do what she was previously doing freely and secretly.

When Moses grows up, the Princess adopts him and he lives in the Egyptian palace. Moses has the best of everything. He's part of the most powerful family in the world and is living in luxury. However, let's consider that the reason Moses has it so good is because Egypt has thousands of slaves. Moses' prosperity is due to the poverty of his own people, something that must have weighed heavily on him. When Moses grows up, he rejects the palace and disowns his adopted family and their corrupt way of life[27].

Moses sees the injustice his own people are facing and knows God has appointed him to do something about it. One day, Moses witnesses an Egyptian mistreating an Israelite. Looking left and right and seeing no one, he murders the Egyptian. Moses made two assumptions. First, he assumed no one saw him kill the Egyptian, but he was wrong. Second, he also assumes that the Israelites will realise that Moses was sent by God to rescue the Israelites.[28] But, the Israelites don't see Moses as their liberator.

The next day, Moses tries to break up a fight between two Israelites and one of them says, "Who made you ruler and judge over us? Are you thinking of killing me as you killed the Egyptian?"[29]

Moses is afraid—the Israelites do not want him as their leader and the King of Egypt wants him dead, so he

---

27   Hebrews 11:24-26
28   Acts 7:25
29   Exodus 2:14

flees from Egypt to the safety of Midian. Moses thought things would work out differently. He thought he would lead Israel to freedom. Things didn't go according to plan and now Moses has made a mess of everything.

Sometimes people chase after their dreams with passion and energy but sadly things don't always work out. Often people pack away their broken dreams and move on with their life. Moses moves on, and he's now married with two sons and is a shepherd. Forty years later, God appears to Moses to rekindle the dream of liberating the people of God from their slavery and speaks to Moses through a burning bush to appoint him to lead God's people to freedom. God is going to redeem the ruins of Moses' life.

When Moses was younger, he was brash and confident, but now that confidence is nowhere to be seen. Moses makes all kinds of excuses and tells God to choose anybody else.[30] What a difference forty years has made! Forty years ago, Moses knew God had appointed him to rescue Israel but, just like Michael Reeves' concussion caused him to forget his wedding, Moses has forgotten his calling. God shows up to remind him that he had been made for this mission, and, while Moses is reluctant and lacking in confidence, he agrees and returns to Egypt. You don't have to be sure or even be confident to be brave. Moses isn't confident but he shows courage by stepping forward in obedience. When you step forward into your calling despite the doubts and difficulties that are ahead, you are brave in the making.

---

[30] Exodus 4:13

A Knockout Wedding

Bible Story: Exodus: 1-4

Press Pause: *Do I believe that God can redeem the ruins of my life?*

Verse to remember:
And we know that God causes everything to work together for the good of those who love God and are called according to his purpose for them.
(Romans 8:28 NIV)

7.

The Never-ending Match

Brave is waiting

It was meant to be just another tennis match on Court 18. It was the opening round of the 2010 Wimbledon Tennis Championships, and Court 18 is not where the big blockbuster matches are played. John Isner wasn't exactly a nobody, he was ranked 19th in the world, but his opponent, Nicholas Mahut was ranked 148th and had earnt his place through pre-tournament qualifying. No one would have predicted this match would go down as one of the great games of all time.

As expected, Isner won the first set 6-4, but Mahut took Isner by surprise taking the second set 6-3. The third set was locked at six games all with Mahut winning it in a tiebreaker, and Isner had his back to the wall. Mahut needed just one more set to clinch an unexpected victory, but Isner fought hard in the fourth set winning it in yet another tiebreaker and the game was now locked at two sets all. The match was headed into a fifth and final set, but it was 9:07 pm and the light on Court 18 was fading, and the match was suspended after almost three hours of play.

Isner and Mahut returned the next day at 2:05 pm. The fifth set reached six games all but with no tiebreaker in the last set, the match continued. Isner had his first match point when he was leading 10-9 but failed to convert the opportunity. Then, on two match points when he was leading 33-32, he again couldn't finish the job.

With the clock at, 5:45 pm Isner and Mahut had set a record for the longest tennis match in history—but they weren't done yet. At 47-47 the scoreboard broke down—it wasn't programmed to go any higher. With Isner leading on 59-58 and within reach of fourth match point he stumbled again tying the match at 59-59. By now it was 9:09 pm and poor light again suspended play. Isner and Mahut had been out on the court for seven hours playing the same set, with the total match time now almost 10 hours. The crowd was on their feet cheering for both players and shouting, "We want more, we want more."

The next day the crowd did get more. Isner and Muhat played for another hour, bringing the total game time to 11 hours 5 minutes over the course of three days. Isner was eventually victorious, winning the final set 70-68. Both players had shown incredible endurance—the last set alone lasted more than eight hours! Isner advanced to the second round where he was visibly exhausted and was profoundly beaten in straight sets, he had nothing left. Isner showed courage not through daring risks but

The Never-ending Match

by his steely determination. It wasn't pretty but he didn't give up.

Likewise, in the Bible we find that David showed great courage by waiting amid very challenging circumstances.

To set the scene:
David is a boy looking after his father's sheep when the prophet Samuel anoints him as the next king of Israel. A little while later David is delivering food to the army when he hears Goliath ridiculing Israel's God. David takes on Goliath and has a giant victory. Everything is going well for David, anything King Saul asks him to do, David does it successfully. Even when Saul appoints David as a commander in his army, Israel is victorious. It isn't long before the women of Israel are singing, "Saul has killed his thousands, and David his ten thousands!"[31]

But, David's big success suddenly becomes a big problem when King Saul becomes jealous. On one occasion David is playing the harp, and Saul hurls a spear at David, but he escapes. Saul is so jealous and fearful of David's success he decides that David must go.

At first, Saul tries flattery. He tells David he is ready to give him his daughter in marriage. Saul had promised that whoever defeated Goliath would marry one of his daughters, but it was a promise Saul never kept. He now promises David he can marry his daughter if he kills 100 Philistines.[32] Saul hopes that David will die in battle but instead David kills 200 Philistines. Giving up all pretence,

---

[31] 1 Samuel 18:7
[32] 1 Samuel 18:25 Saul asks for 100 philistine foreskins which isn't exactly at the top of everyone's wish list!

Saul announces that he wants David dead leaving him no choice but to flee for his life. The Prophet Samuel may have anointed David as the next King of Israel, but David has found himself on the run from the current king.

One time while searching for David with murderous intent, the king takes a toilet break—choosing the very cave where David was hiding. David's men whisper to him,[33] "Now's your opportunity!" David could kill Saul right now and become king by force, but David says no. God has appointed Saul to be king and he will remain king as long as God wants. God has promised David that he will be king one day but today David waits.

David shouts out to Saul:

> Why do you listen to the people who say I am trying to harm you? This very day you can see with your own eyes it isn't true. For the Lord placed you at my mercy back there in the cave. Some of my men told me to kill you, but I spared you.[34]

Saul confesses to David:

> You are a better man than I am, for you have repaid me good for evil.[35]

But, he soon forgets his words and it isn't long before Saul and his army are searching the countryside and trying to kill David once again. Another time David finds Saul and his men asleep, and once again has the opportunity to kill Saul but declines. It was the Lord who promised David

---

33   1 Samuel 24:4
34   1 Samuel 24:9-10
35   1 Samuel 24:17

The Never-ending Match

he would be king one day and David will wait for God to fulfil His promise—he will not try to fulfil God's promise in his timing.

Once again Saul admits his guilt, saying:

> I have sinned. Come back home, my son, and I will no longer try to harm you, for you valued my life today. I have been a fool and very, very wrong.[36]

But, knowing Saul's words can't be trusted, David continues to hide in the wilderness.

We don't know exactly how long David was in the wilderness. Some estimates suggest David was on the run for eight years—longer than the time it takes to complete high school. Just imagine if you had to leave town for eight years because someone had it in for you. David didn't know when his ordeal would end, and it must have felt like it would go on forever.

After many years spent waiting, Saul dies, and David can safely return to Israel. He becomes the leader over the region of Judah, but has another seven years of waiting before he becomes the King of all Israel. It's thought that David was just a teenager when Samuel anointed him as Saul's successor, but he is almost 40 when he finally becomes king over all Israel.

People usually hate waiting. We hate being stuck in traffic, or waiting for a friend to text back, and often become frustrated when things don't happen as fast as they should. Bravery isn't always running into burning buildings

---
[36] 1 Samuel 26:21

or slaying dragons. Sometimes bravery is the slow determination to see a job through to completion, or to stand your ground for your principles, or to keep fighting for justice no matter how hard or how long the road may be. Waiting is very common in the Bible: Moses spends 40 years waiting in the wilderness before God calls him to lead Israel to freedom, Joseph waits years in a prison cell before being elevated to the palace, and Abraham is promised descendants as numerous as the stars but waits decades to see his first child come into the world.

Being brave is waiting for God to fulfil His promises rather than impatiently taking matters into your own hands. If David killed Saul, he could have become king sooner, but it would have been a foolish mistake. He would have spent his reign leading a divided kingdom, fending off revenge attacks from those loyal to Saul. Some are willing to abandon their principles in order to get what they want but David was different. David wanted to be a godly king and refused to take short cuts at the expense of his character. The best way to ensure he would be godly as king was to be godly before he was king. David wouldn't become king through violence or craftiness, but instead trusted God and waited on God to fulfil His promises in His timing.

Brave is waiting.

The Never-ending Match

Bible Story: David is anointed King in 1 Samuel 16. Saul dies at the end of the book of 1 Samuel.

Press Pause: *Am I taking matters into my own hands rather than waiting on God?*

Verse to remember:
> Wait patiently for the LORD. Be brave and courageous. Yes, wait patiently for the LORD. (Psalm 27:14)

8.

Australia's Got Talent

Brave is staying focused

I was 18 when I moved to Ballarat, Victoria to study teaching at university. I quickly made friends with Jared, who lived locally and was a very fit runner. One day after class, Jared asked me if I wanted to go for a run with him. I was happy enough to go for a short jog, but it soon dawned on me that Jared and I had different definitions of 'short' and 'jog'. We ran for about eight kilometres at what seemed a frantic pace to me, though perhaps to Jared was simply jogging.

At the end of the 8km circuit, I was completely exhausted having spent every ounce of energy I possessed just to keep up. I was lying on the ground, puffing and panting, only for Jared to ask, "Want to go for another lap?" I went home, but Jared ran the course again. I guess that's why he would become an Olympic Gold medallist.

In 2008, Jared Tallent burst onto the Olympic scene with a bronze medal in the 20km Men's Race Walk. He backed up that performance with a Silver medal in the men's 50km event just days later. Then at the 2012 Olympics in London, Tallent completed the 50km walk in 3 hours 36 minutes to win another Silver medal. However, it was difficult for him to accept the result as he had long suspected the winner of being a drug cheat.

It took four long years, but eventually Tallent was vindicated. When the athlete who had taken first place was disqualified and his results declared invalid Tallent was awarded the Gold medal and became the Olympic record holder. It had been a long walk to Gold. Jared returned for his third Olympics in 2016, winning a Silver medal in the men's 50km Race Walk, his fourth Olympic medal.

In our university days, Jared didn't often go out partying with the other university students. He was extremely focused on the sport of race walking, not letting anything else distract him from being the best he could be at his chosen path. He also didn't let the actions of other people, or his own disappointment, interfere with the task at hand, putting everything else aside and soldiering on.

Being brave isn't always about embarking on brand new adventures. Sometimes being brave means staying focused on your one God-given task. Jared Tallent was focused on his Olympic dream and couldn't afford to be distracted. Likewise, in the Bible Joshua had to remain focused in order to achieve his God-given goal.

Australia's Got Talent

To set the scene:
Joshua has been appointed to lead God's people, the Israelites. He grew up in Egypt where the Israelites have been oppressed for hundreds of years. God uses Moses to lead God's people out of Egypt, and Joshua witnesses the powerful plagues that God uses to force the Egyptians to let the Israelites go. He witnesses the Red Sea parting and the Israelites walking across on dry ground, and is one of the spies who Moses sends into the promised land. Upon returning, the spies report that the land is very good.

However, they also warn their enemies are strong and their cities are fortified and secured. These spies have witnessed God's power during the plagues of Egypt, but they seem to have forgotten what they saw. They spread fear throughout God's people saying "We can't go up against them! They are stronger than we are!"[37] Only two spies dare to speak positively, Joshua and Caleb. They plead with Israel:

> The land we travelled through and explored is a wonderful land! And if the Lord is pleased with us, he will bring us safely into that land and give it to us. It is a rich land flowing with milk and honey. Do not rebel against the Lord, and don't be afraid of the people of the land. They are only helpless prey to us! They have no protection, but the Lord is with us! Don't be afraid of them![38]

Joshua hasn't forgotten the might and power of God.

Despite Joshua and Caleb's strong words, Israel doesn't trust God enough to enter the land. God sends the

---
[37] Numbers 13:31
[38] Numbers 14:7-9

Israelites back into the wilderness, saying:

> Because your men explored the land for forty days, you must wander in the wilderness for forty years—a year for each day, suffering the consequences of your sins.[39]

Joshua was brave and ready to enter God's promised land. But now he must spend 40 years wandering through the wilderness waiting for the next opportunity. Forty years is a long time and many of Israel's leaders pass away, including Moses who had led Israel for four decades. Joshua is ready to lead a new generation of Israelites into the land God had promised.

The first city that stands in Israel's way is Jericho, a city with strongly fortified walls. There are numerous war tactics that Joshua could use to attack a fortified city. Archers could shoot flaming arrows over the walls, the Israelites could try to enter via a water tunnel, or they could build siege ramps to damage the city walls until they give way. Before the battle, God gives Joshua specific instructions on how to attack the city of Jericho. These instructions are highly unconventional:

> You and your fighting men should march around the town once a day for six days. Seven priests will walk ahead of the Ark, each carrying a ram's horn. On the seventh day you are to march around the town seven times, with the priests blowing the horns. When you hear the priests give one long blast on the rams' horns, have all the people shout as loud as they can. Then the walls of the town will collapse, and the people can charge straight into the town.[40]

---

[39] Numbers 14:34
[40] Joshua 6:3-5

Australia's Got Talent

Joshua has an army of 600,000 troops at his disposal—and God wants them to walk around in circles. The Israelites could dig trenches, build weapons, and do battle but God tells them to keep walking, step after step, until God brings about the victory. The citizens of Jericho watch as the army of Israel approaches as if to attack their city, but all they do is walk around the walls once and return to camp. For six days Israel does the same thing: circle step by step around the city and return to camp. The citizens of Jericho must find this sight quite absurd—these Israelites aren't fighting, they're just going for a walk.

Then, on the seventh day, something puzzling takes place. The Israelites take a second lap, followed by a third and a fourth. Also new is the priests blowing their horns, blasting out some of Israel's favourite tunes. After seven laps of the city the priests still find enough breath for one long blast of the rams' horn. The people of Israel shout as loud as they can and suddenly the walls of Jericho come crashing down. Joshua has led Israel to victory not thanks to their army, or through conventional military tactics, but because of their attentiveness to God's instructions.

Jared Tallent rose to the top of race walking because he dedicated himself to focussing solely on one sport. While other people were socialising or letting themselves get caught up in the distractions around them, Tallent was plodding away, step by step, on his way to Olympic glory. Joshua's success as a leader came from his focus and dedication to following God's instructions. When he was attentive to God's instructions, he had great success.

To be a brave leader you don't need great resources,

experience, skills, or technology. You don't need to be good with words or have a strong personality to make a difference. What you need is great obedience in following God's instructions, step by step until you cross the finish line, and the job is done.

Bible Story: Joshua 6

Press Pause: *Am I getting distracted by many things instead of focusing on my one God-given task?*

Verse to remember:
> The Lord says: "I will guide you along the best pathway for your life. I will advise you and watch over you." (Psalm 32:8)

9.

Transformed by Trouble

Brave is trusting God on bad days

Kim Brennan was a young athlete with a dream of competing in the Olympic Games. Brennan was a gifted hurdler winning the Australian junior championships in the 2001-2002 season when she was just 16 years of age. Leading up to the 2004 Olympics, Brennan was the second-fastest hurdler in Australia over 400 metres. But, before she could book a flight to the Olympics, tragedy struck, and Brennan's Olympic campaign was derailed by injury when she developed a stress fracture in her foot. She started rehabilitation to try to get herself right, but the injury kept reoccurring until it became obvious that she couldn't run anymore. Kim Brennan's athletic career was over at just 19 years old.

As part of Brennan's rehabilitation program, she used a

rowing machine to keep fit. While she wasn't able to run, rowing was something she could do and in time she was encouraged to try rowing on the water. Initially, she wasn't brilliant, commenting, "I went from being one of the best runners in the country to being an absolute Gumby in a rowing boat."[41]

But after just three years of rowing, Brennan was selected to attend the 2008 Olympic games. She returned to the Olympics four years later to claim a bronze medal in Single Sculls and a Silver medal in Double Sculls. Then in 2016, at her third Olympics, Kim Brennan won a Gold medal in Single Sculls and carried the flag for Australia at the closing ceremony.

I imagine Brennan would have been devastated when her injuries ended her hurdling career. She may have felt like her sporting career was over and her dreams ruined. But I wonder if in hindsight she's now grateful because this adversity guided her towards rowing.

Brennan's plans were transformed by trouble. In the Bible, we meet Joseph whose plans were also transformed by trouble, but his came from his jealous brothers.

To set the scene:
Joseph's father, Jacob, has 12 sons, but Joseph is his favourite. Jacob isn't shy about his favouritism either, giving Joseph a beautiful robe of many colours. Joseph's brothers get the message, Jacob loves Joseph more—and they hate Joseph for it. But, when God sends dreams to Joseph, he is happy to tell his brothers all about it, telling

---

[41] 2XU Interview with Kim Crow https://www.2xu.com/uk/crossing-over.html

them:

> We were out in the field, tying up bundles of grain. Suddenly my bundle stood up, and your bundles all gathered around and bowed low before mine![42]

You don't need a doctorate in dream interpretation to work out that the dream is suggesting Joseph's brothers will serve him. Later, Joseph has another dream, and he proudly announces, "The sun, moon, and eleven stars bowed low before me!"[43]

Again, it's not difficult to work out what this dream means, especially given Joseph has eleven brothers. Jacob's favouritism has already made Joseph's brothers bitter towards him, and blabbing about his dreams only made things worse.

One day, Jacob sends Joseph to report back on how his brothers are managing his flocks. When his brothers see him coming, they speak of killing him.

> "Here comes the dreamer!" they said. "Come on, let's kill him and throw him into one of these cisterns. We can tell our father, 'A wild animal has eaten him.' Then we'll see what becomes of his dreams!"[44]

Joseph's brothers rip off his colourful robe and throw him down the well. His brothers sit down to eat, close enough that they can hear him down there. We don't know exactly what Joseph says to them but years later the brothers remembered: "We saw his anguish when

---
[42] Genesis 37:7
[43] Genesis 37:9
[44] Genesis 37:19-20

he pleaded for his life, but we wouldn't listen."[45]

Suddenly, a caravan of camels arrives carrying a group of Ishmaelite traders. One of Jacob's sons, Judah, has a bright idea. What's the point of killing him when they could sell him to these Ishmaelite traders? This way they get rid of Joseph, and they make some money on the side—it's a win-win for Joseph's brothers. The Ishmaelite traders take Joseph to Egypt, and his brothers tell Jacob that Joseph has been killed by a wild animal.

Joseph begins a new life as a slave in Egypt, serving Potiphar, the captain of the palace guard. Initially, Joseph has great success when Potiphar notices that God is with Joseph and promotes him to be his personal attendant. Perhaps Joseph's dreams of becoming a great leader are starting to come true. But trouble arises for Joseph when Potiphar's wife takes a liking to Joseph. "Come and sleep with me,"[46] she demands.

Joseph shows his integrity and refuses, saying:

> My master trusts me with everything in his entire household. No one here has more authority than I do. He has held back nothing from me except you, because you are his wife. How could I do such a wicked thing? It would be a great sin against God.[47]

Potiphar's wife has no such integrity, though, and continues to pursue Joseph. He avoids her as much as he can but one day, she grabs his cloak and Joseph flees. Becoming angry, she falsely accuses Joseph of wrongdoing

---

[45] Genesis 42:21
[46] Genesis 39:7
[47] Genesis 39:8-9

and Potiphar takes swift action and throws Joseph into prison.

Joseph once had dreams of becoming a great leader but since then he's had nothing but trouble. The Bible has an encouraging verse for anyone going through a hard time like Joseph.

> But the Lord was with Joseph in the prison and showed him his faithful love.[48]

God isn't just with us on the good days. God is with us just as much in our worst moments, on days filled with trouble and tragedy.

Joseph continues to show his leadership qualities and soon enough, the prison warden puts him in charge of everything that happens in the prison. One morning, Joseph finds two of the prisoners looking worried. Both men are former officials of the King, one the King's baker, the other his cupbearer. The two men are having troubling dreams but don't know what they mean.

> "Interpreting dreams is God's business," Joseph tells them. "Go ahead and tell me your dreams."[49]

Joseph accurately interprets both of their dreams. It's good news for the cupbearer, he gets his old job back, but not such good news for the baker. Joseph tells him the King will have him put to death and, sure enough, three days later he is executed. Joseph asks the cupbearer to put in a good word for him to the King:

---

[48] Genesis 39:21
[49] Genesis 40:8

Please remember me and do me a favour when things go well for you. Mention me to Pharaoh, so he might let me out of this place. For I was kidnapped from my homeland, the land of the Hebrews, and now I'm here in prison, but I did nothing to deserve it.[50]

But the cupbearer forgets all about him and Joseph is left to spend the next two years in prison.

One morning Pharaoh, the King of Egypt, has two troubling dreams. First, he dreams of seven fat healthy cows being eaten by seven scrawny thin cows. He then dreams of seven fat heads of grain being swallowed by seven withered heads of grain. Pharaoh asks all the magicians and wise men of Egypt what these dreams mean but no one can help him. That's when the cupbearer remembers Joseph. Pharaoh sends for Joseph and, in an instant, Joseph is transferred from the prison to the palace!

God enables Joseph to interpret the Pharaoh's dreams, and he explains they both have the same meaning. There will be seven good years for farming where food will be plentiful, but seven years of famine will follow. Joseph warns Pharaoh that the years of famine will be so severe that people will forget all about the good years.

Joseph makes a suggestion: Store away plenty of food in the good years so that when the bad years arrive there will be food for everyone. Pharaoh decides to appoint Joseph to carry out this very task, and just like that Joseph is elevated to second in charge over all the land of Egypt. It has taken many years, but Joseph's dreams have been fulfilled, his life transformed by trouble.

---

[50] Genesis 40:14-15

Transformed By Trouble

When the years of famine finally arrive, Joseph's brothers come to Egypt because they've heard there is food available. In the end, Joseph's brothers bow before Joseph just as he had dreamed, and Joseph is able to reconcile and reunite with his brothers.

Joseph tells them:

> You intended to harm me, but God intended it all for good. He brought me to this position so I could save the lives of many people.[51]

Perhaps you have experienced trouble and tragedy and wonder how anything good can come from it. God is so powerful that He can take your ruins and turn them into redemption, He can take what's bad and use it for good.

Bible Story: Genesis 37, 39-45

Press Pause: *Do I trust that God can transform my trouble?*

Verse to remember:
God is our refuge and strength, always ready to help in times of trouble. (Psalm 46:1)

---

[51] Genesis 50:20

10.

A Blind Date

Brave is showing generosity to your enemies

Eugene Peterson was a Presbyterian minister and an author. He is probably best known for writing the Message Bible, a paraphrase of the Bible written in contemporary language. Peterson told the story of a time in school when he encountered a second-grade bully by the name of Garrison Johns. Peterson was raised in a Christian home and had learned Bible verses such as 'bless those who persecute you' and 'turn the other cheek'[52].

Somehow Garrison Johns knew this and had chosen to pick on Peterson. Every day after school, Johns would find Peterson and beat him up, also taunting Peterson about his faith, calling him 'Jesus sissy'. Each day Peterson returned home from school bruised and humiliated. His mother told him this had always been the way for Christians in

---
52 See Matthew 5:38-44

the world and urged him to get used to it and to pray for his enemies. Peterson loved going to school but dreaded seeing Garrison Johns.

One day after school Johns found Peterson and proceeded to begin jabbing him. Something snapped in Peterson and all of a sudden, those Bible verses disappeared from Peterson's mind. Grabbing Johns, something that was completely out of character, Peterson was surprised to discover that he was stronger than his tormentor. Wrestling Johns to the ground, he sat on his chest and pinned his arms down with his knees. Johns was now at Peterson's mercy; this was too good to be true! Peterson hit him in the face with his fists, it felt good, so he hit him again, blood spurting out from his nose. By this time other children had gathered around and were cheering Peterson on, encouraging him to blacken Johns' eyes and bust his teeth.

Peterson commanded Johns, "Say Uncle." This is an American way of admitting defeat, and Garrison Johns wasn't about to say it. So, Peterson hit him again, bringing more blood and more cheering. Suddenly, Peterson remembered his Christian training.

Peterson told Johns, "Say I believe in Jesus Christ as my Lord and Saviour." When he wouldn't, Peterson hit him again before trying a second time.

"Say I believe in Jesus Christ as my Lord and Saviour." This time John said it! Peterson said, "Garrison Johns was my first Christian convert." [53]

---

[53] https://www.christiancentury.org/article/2012-03/my-first-convert

A Blind Date

None of us like having enemies, and if we are offered opportunity to take revenge on them it sometimes gets the better of us. During the time of the prophet Elisha the Israelites faced an enemy in the Arameans.

To set the scene:
The Arameans regularly raid the land of Israel, stealing cattle, taking prisoners, and ultimately seeking to invade Israel completely. God protects Israel by telling the prophet Elisha all the plans of Aram's King. The King of Aram makes plans, telling his military officers to set up a base at a certain location. Knowing exactly what they are going to do, Elisha can tell Israel's king what defensive actions to take.

The King of Aram is angry that the enemy always seems to know what he is going to do before he does it, and he confronts his officers to accuse them of leaking his plans.

> Which of you is the traitor? Who has been informing the king of Israel of my plans?[54]

The officers know that the problem is the prophet Elisha, and tell the king:

> Elisha, the prophet in Israel, tells the king of Israel even the words you speak in the privacy of your bedroom![55]

The King of Aram decides there's a simple solution—seize Elisha and lock that troublemaker up. Discovering that Elisha is staying in the town of Dothan, the king sends a large army, a great show of strength to arrest one man.

---
54 2 Kings 6:11
55 2 Kings 6:12

When Elisha's servant wakes up the next morning all he can see are horses, chariots, and troops everywhere.

> "Oh, sir, what will we do now?" the young man cries to Elisha.[56]

Elisha isn't worried; he can see more than his servant can. Elisha prays that his servant can truly see, and the eyes of his servant are opened. He now sees that while there's a human army surrounding the city, an angelic army is surrounding them. As the Aramean army charges forward, Elisha prays for them to be blinded. Soon, the servant can see but the army is blind.

Elisha tells this sightless army:

> You have come the wrong way! This isn't the right city! Follow me, and I will take you to the man you are looking for.[57]

Elisha takes them on a 20km walk to the city of Samaria. Samaria is the capital city of Israel, and it's the last place the Aramean army would want to be. Elisha takes them into the city and asks God to restore their sight, and when the soldiers open their eyes, they discover they're in the middle of Samaria at the mercy of Israel's forces.

In recent times, the Arameans have had the upper hand over Israel. All of a sudden, the tables have turned, and now Israel is perfectly placed to take revenge. When the King of Israel sees that the enemy army is helpless, he can't believe his luck. Like Eugene Peterson, he almost

---

[56] 2 Kings 6:15
[57] 2 Kings 6:19

A Blind Date

feels like it is too good to be true!

He calls to Elisha:

> My father, should I kill them? Should I kill them?[58]

Most people would say yes—after all, if the roles were reversed and the King of Aram had the opportunity, he wouldn't hesitate to kill Israel's troops. Elisha, however, believes there's a better way.

He answers the King:

> Of course not! Do we kill prisoners of war? Give them food and drink and send them home again to their master.[59]

Elisha has offered a strange answer to the King. How should Israel treat their enemies? Bless them. The Arameans would regularly raid Israel, steal their cattle, kidnap their citizens, and were constantly plotting Israel's downfall. It was the Arameans who had come to Israel and gone into the town of Dothan seeking Elisha's arrest. They didn't come to bless Israel, and if they are released, there's every chance they'll attack Israel again.

If following God is important to us, then it should make a difference in our day to day lives. If our actions and choices are just the same as everybody else's, what difference is following God making in our lives? God chose Israel to demonstrate to the nations of the world what God is like. If Israel, the people of God, take revenge on the Arameans just like the Arameans would on them, what makes the

---

[58] 2 Kings 6:21
[59] 2 Kings 6:22

people of God special? How does revenge show God's love to the world?

The King of Israel doesn't simply feed the enemy; he prepares a great feast for the Arameans. Imagine preparing a party with streamers, cake, and music for your most hated enemy. Imagine being the Arameans. They walk into a room, not sure if they'll be beaten or beheaded, but instead they find tables prepared for them with all kinds of food and drinks. Is it a trick? Why are they doing this? Israel's generosity has an impact—after that the Arameans, at least for a time, stay away from Israel. Paul writes in the book of Romans:

> For since our friendship with God was restored by the death of his Son while we were still his enemies.[60]

Once we were like the Arameans; we were God's enemies rebelling against His kingdom. We paid no attention to God and did our own thing. God responded to us with generous love. While we were rebelling, Christ gave up his life to save us. It's this generous love that has transformed the lives of millions of believers right around the world for hundreds of years. As recipients of this generous love, how should we treat our enemies?

Eugene Peterson knew the answer as a young boy:

> You have heard that it was said, 'Love your neighbour and hate your enemy.' But I tell you, love your enemies and pray for those who persecute you.[61]

---

[60] Romans 5:10
[61] Matthew 5:43-44

A Blind Date

God's people are meant to be different, and we should treat our enemies with the same generous love that God has shown us. Be like Elisha and bless your enemies with generous love.

Peterson, in his later years, moved back to the area where he grew up. One day he walked past the spot where he fought with Garrison Johns and obtained his conversion by force. Peterson wondered, whatever had become of Garrison Johns? He opened the phone book and, sure enough, his name was still listed there as living in the local area. Peterson asked himself, "Should I call him?" Would he even remember? And would he still be a bully?" When we display God's generous love to those who hurt us, maybe today's enemies will become tomorrow's friends.

Bible Story: 2 Kings 6:8-23

Press Pause: *How could I show God's love to my enemies?*

Verse to remember:
>Don't repay evil for evil. Don't retaliate with insults when people insult you. Instead, pay them back with a blessing. That is what God has called you to do, and he will grant you his blessing. (1 Peter 3:9)

11.

The Wife Carry

Brave is uncomfortable

Singleton is a small town in New South Wales that is home to the Australian Wife Carrying Titles. Playing this game requires a man to carry his wife over his shoulders while completing an obstacle course.

After the starting gun has fired, you will witness men climbing over hay bales, jumping into mud pits, and scaling fences, all with their partners hanging on for their lives. The couple that completes all the obstacles in the fastest time is the winner and will be crowned Australia's Wife Carrying Champions. Hopefully, their marriage is still intact at the end of the race as the major prize is an all-expenses-paid trip to Finland to compete in the Wife Carrying World Championships. Whoever is crowned the World Champion wins their wife's weight in beer.

The sport of wife-carrying originated in Finland, dating back to the 19th century when robbers would attack a village and steal food, animals, and wives by carrying them over their shoulders. Not the most comfortable journey. According to the International Wife Carrying Competition Rules all participants must enjoy themselves—which is probably easier for the men than for the women. Perhaps Australia's GOAT in this sport is Anthony Partridge who has won the Australian Wife Carrying Championship a record four times—with two different partners!

As we read the stories of brave people in the Bible, we see that they rarely had comfortable experiences.

The first mother we meet in the New Testament isn't Mary but rather her cousin Elizabeth.

To set the scene:
Elizabeth is married to a priest called Zechariah. Priests serve at the temple in Jerusalem twice a year, for a week at a time. Serving in the temple is a big occasion for a priest but even more special is the burning of incense while people pray. The job of burning incense is decided by casting lots, which is a bit like rolling dice, and it's Zechariah who is chosen. This is a big deal, the highlight of his career, as priests were only allowed to burn incense once—it was literally a once-in-a-lifetime opportunity.

Zechariah and his wife Elizabeth are righteous people who follow the Lord completely. Yet, they also have faced disappointment; they had no children. Zechariah and Elizabeth have prayed and prayed for a child, but these prayers have seemingly gone unanswered—and now they are old.

Zechariah is in the temple sanctuary performing his once-

The Wife Carry

in-a-lifetime role when an angel appears to him.

> Don't be afraid, Zechariah! God has heard your prayer. Your wife, Elizabeth, will give you a son, and you are to name him John.[62]

Could this day get any better? A once-in-a-lifetime gig in the temple plus a long-awaited answer to prayer. But Zechariah can't believe it.

> Zechariah says to the angel, "How can I be sure this will happen? I'm an old man now, and my wife is also well along in years."[63]

The angel replies:

> I am Gabriel! I stand in the very presence of God. It was he who sent me to bring you this good news! But now, since you didn't believe what I said, you will be silent and unable to speak until the child is born. For my words will certainly be fulfilled at the proper time.[64]

Being a priest, Zechariah knows all about Gabriel. Gabriel appears in the Old Testament Book of Daniel, which was written about 500 years earlier. Gabriel had told Daniel there will be a time of waiting before God's chosen leader arrives—he was talking about Jesus.

The angel is saying to Zechariah, "I'm the Gabriel you talk about in your sermons and your Bible studies. I've been telling people about Jesus' coming for more than 500 years and because you didn't believe me you forfeit

---

[62] Luke 1:13
[63] Luke 1:18
[64] Luke 1:19-20

the right to talk about it."

Zechariah is silenced because of his lack of belief. It might seem harsh, but Zechariah could have done better; as a priest it shouldn't be difficult for him to believe that God can answer prayer. Zechariah claims he is too old, but so was Abraham. Zechariah would have told people the story of Abraham and Sarah, giving birth to a son in their old age, again and again. Six different times in the Old Testament God opens a barren womb, so why not a seventh?

Zechariah is disciplined by Gabriel, but he learns from the experience. When Elizabeth gives birth to a baby boy everyone wants to know what his name will be. Everyone is expecting the child to be called Zechariah after his father, but Elizabeth insists his name will be John as per Gabriel's instructions. In one of the more comical moments in Scripture, they gesture to Zechariah to ask him what the child's name will be. Comical because Zechariah is mute, he's not deaf! He asks for a writing tablet, which sounds like an iPad but was far less sophisticated, and he writes, "His name is John." Instantly, Zechariah can speak again, and he praises God, prophesying that his son will prepare the way for Jesus.

A few months later the angel Gabriel also visits Mary.

> Greetings, favoured woman! The Lord is with you![65]

As is often the case upon seeing an angel, Mary is alarmed.

> "Don't be afraid, Mary," the angel tells her, "for you have

---
[65] Luke 1:28

The Wife Carry

> found favour with God! You will conceive and give birth to a son, and you will name him Jesus."[66]

Gabriel has been talking about Jesus' arrival for over 500 years and Mary is the chosen mother!

Mary is confused and responds:

> But how can this happen? I am a virgin.[67]

Mary's response might seem similar to Zechariah's but there are some big differences. Zechariah had prayed for a child, Mary had not—she wasn't even married yet. There are precedents in the Bible for old people or barren people giving birth but there's no precedent for what Mary is about to experience.

Finally, Mary's attitude is different because she says:

> I am the Lord's servant. May everything you have said about me come true.[68]

It takes courage to accept God's will, God's way.

God had been planning to send Jesus for hundreds of years, but why did God choose to do it in this uncomfortable way? While Gabriel's promise to Mary is amazing, it also makes her life extremely difficult. She isn't married but pregnant, a scandal in Mary's day. People would have assumed the worst. I'm not sure many people would have believed her when she told them: "God did it."

---

[66] Luke 1:30-31
[67] Luke 1:34
[68] Luke 1:38

When Jesus grows up, a group of people bring to him a woman who is caught in the act of adultery, and they want to put her to death[69]. Jesus protects the woman, but this story gives you an idea of how they felt about her actions. If that's how people felt about an adulterous woman, how do you think people feel about Mary?

We know how Joseph, her fiancée, felt about it—he decides to call off the wedding! Joseph is angry; possibly her entire community is angry—and it's not even Mary's fault.

After an angel appears to Joseph to tell him that Mary is telling the truth, Joseph marries Mary and takes her with him to Bethlehem, as Joseph is required to go to Bethlehem for a census. Australia has a census every five years where we fill out a form, but in Joseph's Day, a census meant every male had to go to their birthplace. What an inconvenience! It is more than 130 kilometres away and Joseph has to walk, and a heavily pregnant Mary travels all that way to Bethlehem with him. That's even more uncomfortable than the Singleton wife carry! The Bible doesn't even say if Mary had a donkey.

Worse, when they finally arrive, there's nowhere for them to stay so Mary gives birth to a baby surrounded by animals, and baby Jesus is put to bed in a feeding trough.

Did it have to be this way? Gabriel has been talking about this event for 500 years so couldn't it have been better planned? Jesus could have been born anywhere, the Taj Mahal, the White House, or at Buckingham Palace like a member of the royal family. England's Prince George was

---

[69] John 8:1-8

The Wife Carry

born in London at St Mary's hospital, ironic given that Mary didn't give birth to the King of Kings in a hospital.

Why did God ask Mary to have this baby before she was married? Why did she have to travel 130 kilometres heavily pregnant? Why a feeding trough? Couldn't God have chosen a more comfortable journey for Mary? And yet we don't see Mary arguing with God. We don't see Mary asking: "What about this? And what will they say? And this isn't fair!" Mary is brave, she accepts God's will, God's way.

When you accept God's will, God's way, you are brave in the making.

Bible Story: Luke chapters 1-2

Press Pause: *Am I willing to accept God's will, God's way?*

Verse to remember:
If any of you wants to be my follower, you must give up your own way, take up your cross, and follow me. (Mark 8:34)

12.

Drilling into Fear

Brave asks for help

The Victorian town of Maryborough, a quiet town of 8000 people, doesn't usually make international headlines. Town GP, Dr. Rob Carson, became a local legend for taking a chance on a highly risky, and most unusual, procedure.

Nicholas, a twelve-year boy, fell off his bike, and sadly he wasn't wearing a helmet. Nicholas got up, complaining of a headache, so his parents took him to the hospital. One minute, Nicholas was talking, the next minute, he was unconscious. Dr. Carson saw the signs of internal bleeding inside the skull placing pressure on Nicholas' brain. Dr. Carson realized that he needed to act fast to relieve the pressure, or Nicholas would surely die. What Dr. Carson needed at that moment was a neurological drill to bore a hole in Nicholas' skull.

The problem was that Maryborough's hospital wasn't equipped with any neurological drills and there wasn't enough time to send Nicholas to the nearest hospital that was. In that moment, Dr. Carson did something unorthodox and extremely gutsy. He turned to the hospital staff and ordered them to "Get me a Black and Decker."[70]

The hospital staff went straight to the maintenance room and grabbed an ordinary household drill, the kind you might have in your shed. Dr. Carson spoke to Nicholas' parents and explained that Nicholas' life was hanging in the balance, and that he only had one shot to save his life. Imagine how scared those parents must have been.

Then Dr. Carson used that household drill to bore a hole in Nicholas' skull. Imagine the thoughts that would have been running through his mind in that moment? Is this in the medical rule book? What if something goes wrong? Does my insurance cover me for using power tools on my patients? What if Nicholas dies? Would there be enough lawyers on earth to save my career? This left-field idea was a massive professional risk for Dr. Carson; if it went wrong, it might have been the last operation he ever performed.

Dr. Carson's brave actions worked; Nicholas' life was saved.

Imagine being Nicholas' parents. One minute you're at home living a normal life, then you're on your way to the hospital to face life and death concerns. The next thing you know, a doctor tells you that your twelve-year-old boy will die unless he takes dramatic action. What would you be feeling in that moment? Would you be afraid?

---

[70] https://www.abc.net.au/news/2009-05-20/doctor-saves-boys-life-with-power-drill/1688618

Drilling Into Fear

One morning, I woke up and found my backdoor wide open. I put this down to clumsiness on my part and thought nothing of it, then I noticed something unusual in the backyard—a basketball cap. I didn't give this much thought at the time either because I was busy getting my daughter ready for school. As I was racing out the door, I grabbed my keys and my phone, but I couldn't find my wallet. Then it hit me; the open backdoor, the strange hat, the missing wallet. I had been robbed. I took my daughter to school, and the moment she was out of the car I hit the phones to try and cancel my bank cards.

I'd assumed this would be a pretty straightforward process but, unfortunately, the person on the other end of the call was not very helpful at all. They asked me question after question about my financial history, most of which I couldn't recall in the heat of the moment. The longer we talked, the greater my anxiety became, and after twenty minutes of these financial quizzes I was told to visit my local bank branch. I was already feeling so stressed, it hadn't been a good start to the day at all. I drove to the bank and walked to the front door, only to find that it was a bank holiday, and they were closed.

Why was I feeling so stressed? Because someone out there had my cards, and I was worried they'd start using them. I was scared that someone was out there taking all my money and I was powerless to stop them. I was anxious because I couldn't see Christ in my chaos.

We all know what it's like to feel fear. An upcoming test, a mystery illness, a loved one in hospital, losing a job—these can all trigger enormous fear. The disciples too, faced a moment of high anxiety one time on the sea of Galilee.

To set the scene:
Jesus tells his disciples:

> Let's cross to the other side of the lake.[71]

Among the disciples are experienced fishermen such as Peter, Andrew, James, and John. Suddenly a huge storm erupts. High waves begin crashing into the boat and it starts filling with water. This is no normal storm; it's throwing experienced fisherman into a panic! One minute everything was fine, the next minute, chaos.

Jesus is sleeping in the boat. Could you sleep in a hurricane? Would you doze off during an earthquake? It's raining, it's pouring, the son of God is snoring. Jesus is sleeping, the disciples are shouting:

> Teacher, don't you care that we're going to drown?[72]

One minute everything was fine, now the disciples are drowning, and Jesus appears to be asleep on the job.

Jesus wakes up and tells the storm to be quiet. Immediately the wind and the waves are completely still. Everything is now calm, except for the disciples who are even more terrified than before.

Jesus asks the disciples an unusual question. He asks:

---
71   Mark 4:35
72   Mark 4:38

Drilling Into Fear

> Why are you afraid?[73]

Why would Jesus ask that? Isn't it obvious? High waves are breaking into the boat, the boat is filling with water, the experienced fishermen thought they were drowning, and Jesus asks, "why are you afraid?" Why wouldn't they be afraid?

If the disciples paid attention only to the wind and waves, they would have every reason to be fearful. But if they instead paid attention to the words of Jesus, they would have looked at the situation differently. What did Jesus tell them?

> Let's cross to the other side of the lake.[74]

Jesus said, "Let us go over to the other side". He didn't say let's go to drown in the middle of the lake. If only the disciples had paid more attention to his words than they did to the wind and the waves. You will be significantly less fearful if you pay attention not to the storm, but to the one who is in the storm with you.

If only they knew who Jesus was. You can tell the disciples don't really know because they ask: "

> Who is this man? ...Even the wind and the waves obey him.[75]

At the beginning of time, Jesus was there with God the Father and the Holy Spirit, creating the world.[76] Jesus was

---
[73] Mark 4:40
[74] Mark 4:35
[75] Mark 4:41
[76] See John 1:1-3

present on the second day of creation making the seas, therefore the seas do not worry him.

Isaiah prophesied about Jesus saying:

> For to us a child is born, to us a son is given, and the government will be on his shoulders. And he will be called Wonderful Counsellor, Mighty God, Everlasting Father, Prince of Peace.[77]

Isaiah describes Jesus as the Prince of Peace. You don't need to worry when the Prince of Peace is in your boat! The fact that the disciples were afraid, demonstrates that they didn't know who he was. I became anxious when I was robbed because I had lost sight of the Prince of Peace. When we drill down into our fear, we find that fear is a result of losing sight of Christ in the chaos. Fear is imagining the future without God in it and forgetting that Christ is in our boat with us.

On the morning I was burgled, I momentarily forgot that my provision, everything I need to live today and every day, comes from God. Jesus promised:

> Seek the Kingdom of God above all else, and live righteously, and he will give you everything you need.[78]

Robbers can take my wallet, but they can never take away my provision which comes from God.

Fortunately, during this time of great anxiety, I had my three-year-old daughter with me. Because she was with

---
[77] Isaiah 9:6
[78] Matthew 6:33

Drilling Into Fear

me, I felt the need to explain to her what was happening, why a police car was visiting our house, and why a detective was dusting for fingerprints.

I told my daughter, "Someone has taken Daddy's wallet but it's going to be okay because Jesus will look after us. He has looked after us in the past and he will keep looking after us in the future." As I reassured my daughter, I reassured myself that the Prince of Peace is in our boat.

I never saw my wallet again, but I only lost a ten-dollar note. I'm very thankful to God we were robbed at night, no one woke up, no one was hurt, and very little was taken.

The disciples panicked in the storm, but they did do one thing right. They woke Jesus up and asked for help. They were totally terrified but at least they took their worries to the right place. Jesus brought peace to the storm and calmed the calamity. He can calm your storms too.

Bible Story: Mark 4:35-41

Press Pause: *Have you lost sight of Christ in your chaos? Are you taking your worries to the right place?*

Verse to remember:
>Give all your worries and cares to God, for he cares about you. (1 Peter 5:7)

13.

Here He Comes

Brave keeps searching

Tim Holding was a Victorian politician. Elected as a Victorian member of parliament at the 1999 state election when he was just 27 years old, he was youthful and confident, articulate, and energetic, and a rising star in his political party. At the age of 30, he received his first ministerial appointment as the Victorian Minister for Manufacturing. A few years later he was promoted, taking on the role of Minister for Police. More responsibilities kept on coming: Minister for Finance, Minister for Water, and Minister for Tourism. Tim Holding was clearly a future leader in the making.

On August 30th 2009, Holding, who was now 37, went hiking on Mount Feathertop, and the next day he was reported missing. It was somewhat ironic that Holding would get lost in the Victorian bush given he was the Victorian Minister for Tourism. He had fallen more than 100 metres down the side of a mountain, and he was lost, injured, and thought he was going to die.

Significant resources were deployed to find and rescue the Minister for Tourism. Victoria Police were deployed, and dispatched helicopters to scour the bushland. A team of 80 people that included members of the SES and the Army were assembled to search for one man. The Australian Federal Police even sent out a spy plane equipped with thermal imaging technology, which was usually used for tracking down terrorists, not government ministers. The Victorian Premier would spare no effort in order to find and rescue his minister. For two days and nights, Holding waited, hoping that someone was looking for him. In the end Holding was found, rescued, and back at work just a few days later.

With the same intensity and tenacity, Jesus looks for us. Here he comes.

To set the scene:
Jesus once asked this question:

> Suppose one of you has a hundred sheep and loses one of them. Doesn't he leave the ninety-nine in the open country and go after the lost sheep until he finds it? And when he finds it, he joyfully puts it on his shoulders and goes home. Then he calls his friends and neighbours together and says, 'Rejoice with me; I have found my lost sheep.' I tell you that in the same way there will be more rejoicing in heaven over one sinner who repents than over ninety-nine righteous persons who do not need to repent.[79]

After calming a storm, Jesus arrives at the other side of the lake. As he climbs out of the boat, a man possessed

---
[79] Luke 15:4-7

by an evil spirit comes out from the tombs to meet him. This man lives in the burial caves and can no longer be restrained, even with a chain. Whenever he is put into chains and shackles—as he often is—he snaps the chains from his wrists and smashes the shackles. No one is strong enough to subdue him. Day and night he wanders among the burial caves and in the hills, howling and cutting himself with sharp stones.[80]

This man is a troubled soul. Let's take a look at his resumé:

- Demon possessed (Mark 5:2)
- Lives in a graveyard (Mark 5:3)
- Breaks chains (Mark 5:4)
- Cuts himself with stones (Mark 5:5)
- Howling (Mark 5:5)

Luke's Gospel also tells us that this man was naked![81] Many people would say this guy is a lost cause. Somewhere, somehow, this man's life went off the rails. His life is a complete mess and yet Jesus comes looking for him. Here he comes.

On another occasion Jesus tells a story about a lost son.

> A man had two sons. The younger son told his father, 'I want my share of your estate now before you die.' So, his father agreed to divide his wealth between his sons. A few days later this younger son packed all his belongings and moved to a distant land, and there he wasted all his money in wild living.[82]

---

[80] Mark 5:2-5
[81] Luke 8:27
[82] Luke 15:11-13

One of the sons in this story rejects his father, takes his money, and leaves without even saying thanks. It doesn't take long before this son finds himself in trouble.

About the time his money ran out, a great famine swept over the land, and he began to starve. He persuaded a local farmer to hire him, and the man sent him into his fields to feed the pigs. The young man became so hungry that even the pods he was feeding the pigs looked good to him. But no one gave him anything.[83]

The son begins to realise how foolish and how stupid he has been. He rejected his father and made a complete pigsty of his life. Serves him right, many would say.

The son realises that even his father's hired workers are better off than he is. He couldn't go back, could he? Not after everything he's done. The son believes it's too much to ask his father to take him back as a son. Instead, he decides to humble himself and apologise to his dad in the hope that he will have him back as a servant.

Jesus told this story so that we might know how God feels about us. All of us have rejected God's wisdom for how we should live our lives at one time or another. All of us have tried to do things our way instead of God's way and, like the son, made a mess of things. How does God feel about us returning to him? How does this father react when he sees his son? Will he give his son a spray, remind him of how he's let the family down? Will he even speak to him?

The son returns home to his father. And while he is still

---
[83] Luke 15:14-16

Here He Comes

a long way off, his father sees him coming. Next thing you know the son can see the father coming. Here he comes. The son is walking back to the father, but the father is running full pelt toward his son. Filled with love and compassion, he reaches his son, embraces him, and kisses him.

The son tries to make a speech about how he's sorry but the father interrupts:

> Quick! Bring the finest robe in the house and put it on him. Get a ring for his finger and sandals for his feet. And kill the calf we have been fattening. We must celebrate with a feast, for this son of mine was dead and has now returned to life. He was lost, but now he is found.[84]

Jesus told this story so you would know there's a God in heaven who comes running after you. Here he comes.

That troubled soul who lives in the graveyard across the lake breaking chains, howling, and screaming. Jesus comes to set him free, and the man is completely healed and restored.

Now consider the disciples. They had risked their lives at sea and had a near-death experience. Why? So, Jesus could help one person. Jesus went across the lake to set one man free and return home. Jesus went all that way to save one person. There was one lost troubled soul over the other side of the lake so here he comes. Jesus was coming in his boat and no amount of wind, rain, thunder and lightning, howling and screaming, graveyards, broken chains, or nudity is going to change Jesus' mind. Here he

---
[84] Luke 15:22

comes across the lake on a mission of mercy.

What Jesus does for this one man is a picture of what he did for all of humanity. Jesus left the comfort of heaven to come to earth and give his life so we might be saved. Here he comes.

Jesus saw that we were spiritually lost, and he couldn't stay at home while we were in trouble. So here he comes. He's searching through the bush for his lost sheep, he's coming by boat across the sea to rescue a troubled soul, and here he comes to rescue you as well. He's sending out the helicopters, he's searching through the bush, he's deploying the police and the Army and the SES, he's launching the spy planes with thermal imaging technology. God is calling on all of His resources and devoting all of His energies for the sake of a mercy mission to rescue you. That's why Jesus came. Here he comes!

Tim Holding was lost and needed rescuing. The troubled soul across the lake was lost and needed rescuing. We were lost and needed rescuing. Jesus came to save each one of us. That's why he died on the cross. Jesus gave his life for all the times you and I have wandered away from God. When we did our very worst, Jesus gave his very best. We wandered away but Jesus came to rescue us because he loves us. Jesus loves you, it's not just words on a page, it's blood on a cross. Here he comes.

Here He Comes

Bible Story: Mark 5:1-20 & Luke 15: 11-32

Press Pause: *Who does God want me to search for?*

Verse to remember:
For the Son of Man came to seek and save those who are lost. (Luke 19:10)

14.

The Fast Lane

Brave is selfless

Ian Thorpe is Australia's most decorated Olympian, the only Australian who has won five Olympic Gold medals. He first announced himself on the world stage by winning the 400 metres freestyle at the 1998 world championships at just 15 years of age. At the Sydney Olympics, Thorpe, now 17, dominated the pool winning three Gold and two Silver medals.

Four years later Australia's swimmers were competing at the Australian championships for a spot on the next Olympic team. Ian Thorpe was a heavy favourite in the men's 400m freestyle, as he was the reigning Gold medallist and world record holder. Thorpe was considered a shoo-in for the Olympic squad; this would be a training run to tune-up for the Olympics later in the year. But as Thorpe lined up on the blocks for the start of the race, the unthinkable happened. As Thorpe was getting into his starting position he overbalanced and fell into the pool before the starter's gun had fired. Thorpe was disqualified and would fail to qualify for a place at the Olympics—despite being the fastest swimmer in the world. Grant Hackett qualified for the first place and the relatively unknown Craig Stevens qualified in second place. Australians could see a Gold medal slipping away, and many wanted Thorpe to be reinstated for the Olympics. The problem was that two Australians had already qualified for the event at the Olympics; there wasn't room for three. Craig Stevens was under a lot of pressure to give up his place so that Thorpe could defend his Gold medal.

Armchair swimming fans might have wanted Stevens to make way for Thorpe, but Stevens had earned his place on the team. He had trained every day in the early hours of the morning, swimming hundreds of kilometres for this opportunity. Stevens had just qualified for his first Olympics and now he was expected to give up his place? Why should he?

However, several weeks later Craig Stevens did indeed give up his spot to allow Ian Thorpe to compete. Ian Thorpe went to the 2004 Athens games and won the Gold medal in the 400m freestyle thanks to the huge sacrifice Stevens had made. Thorpe ended up becoming Australia's most successful Olympian, and went on to become famous, had a swimming pool named in his honour, hosted television shows, and received honorary doctorates. Stevens went to the 2004 Olympics and swam in a relay team winning a Silver, his only Olympic medal. He doesn't live a life of fame, and today he's a swimming coach investing in the next generation of Australian swimmers. But Stevens will be best remembered for his selflessness gifting Thorpe a Gold medal.

The Fast Lane

Being brave sometimes results in fame and acclaim, but sometimes it means allowing the spotlight to pass you by. John the Baptist was brave in this second way.

To set the scene:
John had a remarkable birth to ageing parents. His father Zechariah, a priest, prophesies that John will prepare the way for God's promised King. John begins preaching and the crowds turn up in big numbers. John boldly urges people to repent of their sin and be baptized, and long lines of people come forward for baptism. People begin to wonder, could this be the person we've been waiting for? Could John be God's promised King?

John ends their speculation, "I am not the Messiah."[85] John doesn't let the praises of the crowd go to his head, telling them:

> I baptize with water, but right here in the crowd is someone you do not recognize. Though his ministry follows mine, I'm not even worthy to be his slave and untie the straps of his sandal.[86]

John knows he has a role to play in God's Kingdom, but he also knows it is not the starring role. Jesus is the star of the show, John is a mere extra in the production. John has the privilege of baptizing Jesus.

At the time he tells Jesus:

> I am the one who needs to be baptized by you.[87]

---
[85] John 1:20
[86] John 1:26-27
[87] Matthew 3:14

John sees God's Spirit descend on Jesus and knows he is God's appointed leader. Sometime later, his followers come to him with a problem. Jesus is baptizing nearby, and everyone is going to him. Crowds for Jesus are growing while John's crowds are declining. This might be a problem for John's followers but it's not a problem for John. John compares himself to the best man at a wedding—it's not his wedding, the best man is just delighted to be there and serve the groom in any way he can.

John says,

> Therefore, I am filled with joy at his success. He must become greater and greater, and I must become less and less.[88]

John is selfless, he knows it isn't about him.

Not all of Jesus' followers share John the Baptist's selfless attitude. Two of his disciples, James and John, approach Jesus wanting a favour. They ask Jesus:

> When you sit on your glorious throne, we want to sit in places of honour next to you, one on your right and the other on your left.[89]

James and John have been watching too many Jewish Messiah movies, and they think that following Jesus will lead to fame and acclaim. James and John are seeking the limelight, they want the book deals, they want millions of Instagram followers, they want a swimming pool named

---

[88] John 3:30
[89] Mark 10:37

after them! John the Baptist said he wasn't worthy to untie Jesus' sandals, yet James and John think they deserve to sit on a throne. Jesus tells them they've got no idea what they're talking about. Jesus explains that leaders in the world are always bossing people around and flaunting their authority. Jesus teaches that truly great leaders are servants, not superstars.

When I was in university, I picked up some work as a school cleaner. Each day after school I would vacuum every classroom, empty the bins, mop, and clean the toilets. I was eager to be a leader that God would use in a big way. I wanted to be a great leader and here I was cleaning the toilets! In hindsight, I consider cleaning to be excellent preparation for leadership. Christian leadership often requires serving when the spotlight isn't on. Sometimes Christian leadership comes with an audience but often it involves serving people in ways no one will ever see. Serving Jesus can be difficult, messy, and sometimes thankless—like my cleaning job. God's Kingdom needs leaders who will faithfully turn up to serve each day...even when no one's watching. People who become leaders just for the spotlight don't last long. Before Jesus' crucifixion, he demonstrated what true leadership looks like.

It was time for supper, and the devil had already prompted Judas, son of Simon Iscariot, to betray Jesus. Jesus knew that the Father had given him authority over everything and that he had come from God and would return to God. So, he got up from the table, took off his robe, wrapped a towel around his waist, and poured water into a basin. Then he began to wash the disciples' feet, drying them with the towel he had around him.[90]

In the first century, people spent considerable time walking on dusty roads in sandals. By the end of a long day of travelling, you would expect to have very dirty feet. The job of foot washing was at the bottom of the barrel, one for the servant with the lowest rank. Unexpectedly, Jesus picks up a towel and starts doing the lowest job. The King of Kings is the servant of all. His disciples can't believe it, Peter isn't sure if he's going to allow it. Jesus washes all his disciples' feet, even Judas who is planning to betray him.

Jesus tells them:

> You call me 'Teacher' and 'Lord,' and you are right, because that's what I am. And since I, your Lord and Teacher, have washed your feet, you ought to wash each other's feet. I have given you an example to follow. Do as I have done to you.[91]

Jesus isn't afraid to get his hands dirty and act selflessly. Not long after washing his disciple's feet, he hangs on a cross laying down his life for them.

Craig Stevens could have kept his Olympics spot and demanded some of the limelight. Instead, Stevens chose to let the world's fastest swimmer take his place. John the Baptist's ministry started with crowds and ended in prison. He was arrested on false charges and later executed by a ruler wanting to keep his family happy. John knew his role was to prepare the way for Jesus. He was to be a selfless servant, not a superstar. When the crowds began leaving

---

90   John 13:2-5
91   John 13:13

The Fast Lane

John to go to Jesus, John was delighted for Jesus to take over. He bravely took a back seat allowing Jesus to have the fast lane.

Bible Story: Mark 10:35-45, John 3:22-30, John 13:1-17

Press Pause: *Am I seeking to be a servant or a superstar?*

Verse to remember:
He must become greater and greater, and I must become less and less. (John 3:30)

15.

Miner Miracle

Brave is praying

On August 5th, 2010, there was a dramatic collapse of a gold mine in Chile that left 33 miners trapped more than 600 metres below the surface. The mine operators didn't know where the miners were or even if anyone was still alive. A rescue team drilled for 17 days, finding nothing they assumed the worst. But as the drill came out of the ground on the 17th day, there was a note attached to the end of the drill. The note said: 'We are well in the shelter, the 33 of us'. For the last 17 days, 33 miners had been living off emergency rations in the underground shelter; each man eating two teaspoons of tuna and one biscuit every two days.

The miners now had a line of communication with the surface and could receive food and other supplies through a 5-inch hole. 5 inches is about 12cm, which is good for sending down food and medicine, but to get the miners out, a large tunnel was needed. It was an incredibly difficult task to drill so far underground without causing the mine to collapse.

It took 69 days to rescue the miners. Imagine being stuck underground for 69 days. That's like missing an entire school term! It's also 69 days without video games, social media, Netflix, mobile phones, or a shower. It must have felt like an eternity waiting underground. The miners didn't know if they would live or die, and no one was sure if the rescue efforts would be successful or not.

There was an unlikely hero called José Henriquez. He was one of the miners trapped below the surface but, more importantly, he was also a follower of Jesus. He started preaching to the miners and reciting the Bible from memory. The miners would gather to pray for their rescue twice a day at 12pm and 6pm, and they would sing songs together like a church. The rescue team sent down 33 small bibles through the 5-inch hole. On the day the men were rescued, the miners wore t-shirts that said 'Gracias Señor' which means 'Thank you, Lord'.

Chilean President Sebastian Pinera said: "When the first miner emerges safe and sound, I hope all the bells of all the churches of Chile ring out forcefully, with joy and hope because faith has moved mountains."[92] All 33 miners were safely rescued. The miners went to work on August 5th and didn't return home until October 13th. This had been an unbelievable escape.

The Chilean President acknowledged this rescue wasn't simply about drilling holes—God had moved miraculously. The t-shirts the miners wore had Psalm 95:4

---

[92] https://uk.reuters.com/article/uk-chile-miners/chiles-trapped-miners-finally-set-to-escape-idUKTRE6980F120101012

Miner Miracle

imprinted on them: 'He holds in his hands the depths of the earth and the mightiest mountains'. The Bible is full of stories of miracles occurring and they often begin with a simple prayer, much like the story of Peter.

To set the scene:
Peter is one of the early followers of Jesus and an important leader in the early Church. He finds himself trapped in a jail cell, as King Herod had arrested and executed the disciple James and when he saw how much this pleased the Jewish people, he arrests Peter as well. Herod is planning to put Peter on trial to win even more popularity from the Jewish people. Peter is being held in prison guarded by four squads of four soldiers each—a quick bit of maths tells us that Peter is being monitored by 16 troops! That's tight security. Peter's only crime is sharing the truth about Jesus; he's done nothing worthy of execution. It's completely unfair but there's nothing anyone can do about it. The only thing the church can do is the most powerful thing of all—they can pray.

Being brave isn't always about slaying dragons and rescuing princesses. Being brave means praying for God to intervene in situations which, humanly speaking, seem impossible. The early church doesn't try to blow up the prison or kidnap Peter—that would be futile and see even more believers in prison. Instead, the church earnestly prays for Peter's freedom. Peter would later write in a letter:

> The eyes of the Lord watch over those who do right, and his ears are open to their prayers.[93]

---
[93] 1 Peter 3:12

As the church prays for Peter, God hears their prayers. It's the night before Peter's trial. The trial is a charade, a kangaroo court. It's not about finding justice—Peter's death has already been decided by Herod. This is meant to be the last night of Peter's life, but Peter is sleeping. If you knew you were going to die tomorrow, how well would you sleep tonight? Peter has every earthly reason to be anxious and yet he has a peace that prevails.

One time, Peter was on a boat with Jesus in the middle of a terrifying storm. Peter was an experienced fisherman, so he was familiar with storms, but this one was off the charts. High waves were crashing into the boat, and it was beginning to fill with water. Jesus was sleeping through the storm—he created the wind and the waves, so they don't worry him.

Peter and the other disciples shouted:

> Teacher, don't you care that we're going to drown?[94]

Jesus woke up and brought calm to the calamity because he was the Prince of Peace. Now, Peter is in prison and doesn't know if he'll live or die, but he still sleeps because he has the Prince of Peace living within him.

Suddenly, there is a bright light, and an angel stands before the sleeping Peter. The angel gives Peter a nudge to wake him, and tells him to get up, and his chains fall from his wrists. Next, the angel tells him to get dressed and put his sandals on—they have places to go. Peter does what he's told but he just thinks it's a dream. They walk

---

[94] Mark 4:38

Miner Miracle

past one set of guards and then another, then they arrive at an iron gate leading into the city. The gate opens all by itself and they walk out of the prison and into the street, when suddenly the angel disappears. Peter now realises this isn't a dream, it's really true and he's standing in the middle of the city completely free. This is an unbelievable escape!

God has intervened miraculously in the middle of an impossible situation to keep Peter alive. Peter now decides to go to the home of Mary, one of the believers. It's good timing, as many believers are meeting there to pray. Peter is about to turn up at his own prayer meeting! He knocks and Rhoda comes to the door. Peter's probably keen to get inside, he is after all a wanted man, but Rhoda is so overjoyed by hearing Peter's voice she runs back to tell the others, leaving poor Peter knocking at the door. Rhoda bursts into the prayer meeting to announce that Peter is standing at the door! The believers react with disbelief, "You're out of your mind!"[95]

Imagine the scene: a group of believers praying together, some sitting, maybe some standing. What would their prayers have sounded like? *"Dear Lord, we pray for your servant Peter, we ask that by your mighty power you would release Peter, set him free from the evil plans of Herod, and send him back to us safely."* Amen, Amen, others in the room would echo and agree. *"Yes, Lord as you saved Shadrach, Meshach, and Abednego from King Nebuchadnezzar and saved them from the fiery furnace we ask that you would save Peter from the plans of King Herod."* More shouts of Amen as the believers agree with

---

[95] Acts 12:15

one another. Yet when the Lord answers their prayers, they don't believe it. What were the believers expecting to happen? Were they hoping for the best but expecting the worst? The believers open the door and Peter tells them the most amazing story about his unbelievable escape.

Like the miners trapped underground you will face many situations in life that are beyond your control. You'll be tempted to try and control them, you'll brainstorm ideas, make plans, and try and get other people to see things your way. Ultimately, you'll come to see, despite your best efforts, that there are many things in this life that are beyond your control. Usually, people become discouraged when they realise they're in a hopeless situation. Christians, however, ought to welcome impossible situations because that's when they will stop relying on themselves and start relying on God.

As believers, prayer should be our first response, not our last resort. God hears the prayers of his followers, and nothing is impossible for him. Brave people ask God for help. Brave people pray.

Bible story: Acts 12:1-19

Press Pause: *Is prayer my first response or last resort?*

Verse to remember:
Don't worry about anything; instead, pray about everything. Tell God what you need and thank him for all he has done. (Philippians 4:6)

16.

Noisy Pirates

Brave is generous

Johnny Depp is a Hollywood megastar. His first acting role was in the film *A Nightmare on Elm Street* in 1984. But Depp is probably best known for playing the role of Jack Sparrow in the Walt Disney film series, *Pirates of the Caribbean*. Depp's acting career has earnt him fame, awards, and enormous wealth. He earned $880 million in 13 years, but, remarkably, it's almost all gone[96].

How in the world did Depp lose so much money?

He owns 14 properties including five apartments in Los Angeles, a chateau in the south of France, and a horse farm in Kentucky. He owns three islands in the Bahamas, an $18 million yacht, 200 pieces of artwork, and he spends $30,000 a month on wine. Depp has a fetish for collecting Hollywood memorabilia, so much so he has 12 storage facilities full of it. He employs a staff of 40, including his own personal doctor, at a cost of $3.6

---

[96] https://www.news.com.au/entertainment/celebrity-life/how-johnny-depp-blew-880-million/news-story/0c2649cba91dc8facc59eea8a9cb5cd8

million a year. He has 45 luxury vehicles and 70 guitars, making him one very noisy pirate.[97]

What if, while sitting on his $18 million yacht strumming his 70 guitars, Captain Sparrow chose to spend a large part of his $880 million educating and feeding hungry children? While we don't all have 12 storage facilities of Hollywood memorabilia, we all store up treasures that we consider valuable. It's reminiscent of a story Jesus told:

> A rich man had a fertile farm that produced fine crops. He said to himself, "What should I do? I don't have room for all my crops." Then he said, "I know! I'll tear down my barns and build bigger ones. Then I'll have room enough to store all my wheat and other goods. And I'll sit back and say to myself, 'My friend, you have enough stored away for years to come. Now take it easy! Eat, drink, and be merry!'"
>
> But God said to him, "You fool! You will die this very night. Then who will get everything you worked for?"
>
> Yes, a person is a fool to store up earthly wealth but not have a rich relationship with God. (Luke 12:16-21 NLT)

Jesus was reminding his listeners that you can spend your life chasing after the wrong wealth. Just like that farmer, we can waste our lives chasing after temporary riches that are worthless the moment we pass away. As Captain Jack Sparrow says, "not all treasure is silver or gold."

The early followers of Jesus took this to heart, and the early Church had an amazing culture of generosity and

---

[97] https://www.vulture.com/2017/05/everything-johnny-depp-wasted-his-money-on.html

giving to those in need.

Acts 4:32:
> All the believers were united in heart and mind. And they felt that what they owned was not their own, so they shared everything they had.

Acts 4:34-35:
> There were no needy people among them, because those who owned land or houses would sell them and bring the money to the apostles to give to those in need.

One of the early Church leaders who sets an example for generosity is Barnabas.

To set the scene:
His first recorded action in the Bible is selling a field and giving the money to the Church. That's a big thing to do, imagine selling your house and giving the money away. Barnabas' generosity isn't limited to giving away money. Barnabas' real name is Joseph, but the believers call him Barnabas because it means 'son of encouragement'. Barnabas is generous with his words, and he loves to encourage people, especially people others look down on.

There is a Jewish religious leader named Saul who violently persecutes Christians. He has believers arrested, tortured, and killed. Here's how Saul describes his opposition to the Church:

> I used to believe that I ought to do everything I could to oppose the very name of Jesus the Nazarene. Indeed, I did just that in Jerusalem. Authorized by the leading

priests, I caused many believers there to be sent to prison. And I cast my vote against them when they were condemned to death. Many times, I had them punished in the synagogues to get them to curse Jesus. I was so violently opposed to them that I even chased them down in foreign cities.[98]

But everything changes when Saul meets Jesus. He is completely transformed, and instead of killing Christians he becomes one! Saul goes to Jerusalem to get to know the believers, but unsurprisingly the believers who know all about this religious terrorist are suspicious of his motives. They don't believe his conversion is genuine, perhaps just another way for him to arrest Christians. It is Barnabas who bravely takes a risk and listens to Saul's miraculous story. Barnabas speaks up for Saul and tells the believers that he really has met the risen Jesus.

Barnabas is described as a man strong in faith, full of God's Spirit and generosity. We know he is generous with his money, his encouraging words, and in giving people a second chance. Barnabas also generously sacrifices his life and comfort for the sake of the good news. Barnabas and Saul travel together sharing the good news of Jesus as missionaries. These aren't easy trips as they are often violently attacked by those seeking to silence them.

Barnabas sets an example to the Church through his generosity and others follow suit, selling fields and giving money to the Church. But not everyone has the same motives as Barnabas. There's a couple in the Church, Ananias and Sapphira. Like Barnabas, they sell some property but unlike Barnabas they keep some of

---
[98] Acts 26:9-11

the proceeds for themselves. In truth there is nothing technically wrong with this, there is no rule about how generous people need to be. Ananias and Sapphira are perfectly free to give all, some, or none of the money to the Church. But Ananias and Sapphira want people to think they were giving away all the money to the Church and that they are generous and sacrificial like Barnabas. So, they make a secret plan, they will keep some of the money but tell the Church leaders they are giving it all away.

Barnabas' generosity in giving the proceeds of a field matched the sacrificial generosity of the rest of his life. Ananias and Sapphira are not genuine, they thought they could fool the Church. They thought they could play the role of generous Christian without the sacrifice. Their actions demonstrate that they care more about what people think than about what God thinks.

Even today we need to be wary of those who show off their faith to impress people, and care more about their image than they do about their relationship with God. Jesus warned us about these people saying:

> Watch out! Don't do your good deeds publicly, to be admired by others, for you will lose the reward from your Father in heaven. When you give to someone in need, don't do as the hypocrites do—blowing trumpets in the synagogues and streets to call attention to their acts of charity! I tell you the truth, they have received all the reward they will ever get.[99]

Jesus teaches his followers to give our gifts privately

---
99 Matthew 6:1-2

so that our only reward will come from our Heavenly Father. If you want to blow trumpets to announce how good you are, it begs the question: Who are you trying to impress? Ananias and Sapphira wanted to blow trumpets so everyone would know how 'Christian' they were. They were just noisy pirates wanting attention and admiration from the Church. God isn't fooled by our pretending, and He certainly wasn't fooled by Ananias and Sapphira.

Peter says to Ananias:

> Ananias, why have you let Satan fill your heart? You lied to the Holy Spirit, and you kept some of the money for yourself. The property was yours to sell or not sell, as you wished. And after selling it, the money was also yours to give away. How could you do a thing like this? You weren't lying to us but to God![100]

God is not impressed when we pretend. Ananias and Sapphira were seeking to infiltrate the Church through their impressive deeds. If they had gotten away with it who knows what damage these two pretenders would have done.

Brave Christians are generous and sacrificial. We use everything we have to advance God's good news. If we have financial resources, we use these wisely and generously to help those in need and help spread the message of God's love, but the generosity of Christians isn't limited to our finances. Brave Christians, like Barnabas, are generous with their money, words, their very lives—and don't need to be noisy about it.

---

[100] Acts 5:3-4

Noisy Pirates

Bible Story: Acts, chapters 4 and 5

Press Pause: *In what ways am I being generous? In what ways am I not?*

Verse to remember:
You should remember the words of the Lord Jesus:
It is more blessed to give than to receive. (Acts 20:35)

17.

Jail House Rock

Brave is finding joy in all circumstances

When I was a teenager, I had a friend who lived in the most unusual house. From the outside it looked like a regular home, but once inside I was taken back in time. It had a retro feel to it, and when I walked into the kitchen, I saw that the entire room was a tribute to the late Elvis Presley. Elvis lived between 1935-1977 and is one of the great musical performers of all time. Even today he is the best-selling solo artist in history. He is known as the 'King of Rock and Roll' or simply as 'The King'.

My friend's kitchen had Elvis' records on the walls, Elvis pictures, and Elvis memorabilia. There was even a jukebox in the kitchen that played Elvis' classic songs such as *Jail House Rock* and *Hound Dog*. I wondered why my friend's kitchen was a memorial to the great Elvis Presley, but then I met my friend's father who bore an uncanny resemblance to the king of rock and roll. Not only was he an Elvis fanatic, he was also an Elvis impersonator. One time he even travelled to the Parkes Elvis Festival. Parkes is a town of 11,000 people in the central west region of New South Wales that is best known for its radio telescope named 'The Dish', which played a role in the Apollo 11 moon landing.

In 1992, Parkes held its first-ever Elvis festival to coincide with his birthday on January 8th. Elvis never visited Parkes, in fact he never toured in Australia at all. Today the Parkes Elvis Festival attracts more than 25,000 people with more than 200 events for people to shake, rattle, and roll their way around. There's the Elvis Street parade with a fleet of vintage 1950's vehicles, a Miss Priscilla competition (a tribute to Elvis' wife), busking competitions, an Elvis tribute show, and there's even a pool party called Viva Splash Vegas. The local churches of Parkes have also been getting in on the action with an Elvis Gospel service celebrating the gospel songs that Elvis loved. It was the Elvis look-a-like competition that inspired my friend's father to travel to Parkes. It involves long lines of men with slick black hair, wearing white capes and sunglasses. They practice their dance moves and recite Elvis' famous phrase: "Thank you, thank you very much."

Christians, too, are impersonators of a king. In the Bible we find two of Jesus followers, Paul and Silas who are proclaiming not the king of rock and roll, but rather Jesus, the King of all Kings.

To set the scene:
Paul and Silas have travelled to the Macedonian city of Philippi and are in new territory, there are no Christians and no churches in this area. Paul and Silas encounter

Jail House Rock

some early success, meeting Lydia, a merchant who becomes a believer in Jesus. Lydia opens her home to Paul and Silas, which then becomes the base for the first Church in Philippi. It's not all smooth sailing for Paul and Silas though.

On one occasion they encounter a slave girl who has become possessed by evil spirits. She follows Paul around shouting, "These men are servants of the Most High God and they have come to tell you how to be saved."[101] She may be demon-possessed but she is also correct. Paul puts up with this for a while but, eventually, he's had enough and confronts the demon. Paul demands, "I command you in the name of Jesus Christ to come out of her."[102]

Instantly Jesus sets her free. This is good news for the slave-girl but it's very bad news for her corrupt owners. They were making good money from her fortune-telling powers and now their business is ruined.

They are furious at Paul and Silas and have them dragged before the authorities.

"The whole city is in uproar because of these Jews!"[103] they shout, even though they had no problem with Paul and Silas until now. "They are teaching customs that are illegal for us Romans to practice."[104]

The real problem is about money, not the customs of Rome.

---

[101] Acts 16:17
[102] Acts 16:18
[103] Acts 16:20
[104] Acts 16:21

It's a similar story later on in Ephesus where the idol makers and silversmiths start a riot because the more people who follow Jesus, the fewer the people that buy idols. These people want to deny the truth in order to protect their business and their wealth. Elvis is known for this quote: "Truth is like the sun, you can shut it out for a time but it ain't going away."

For proclaiming the truth about Jesus, Paul and Silas are stripped naked and beaten with wooden rods. After being severely beaten they are thrown into prison where their feet are clamped in the stocks. Paul and Silas are battered and bruised but their spirits are not broken. At around midnight Paul and Silas are praying and singing hymns to God, and the other prisoners are listening! Of course, the other prisoners are listening, what choice did they have?

It's midnight in a Philippi jail and Paul and Silas are doing the original jailhouse rock! They are giving praise to the King above all kings and the other prisoners can do little else but listen. Paul and Silas had their clothing taken away, they've lost some skin as well, and their freedom has been taken from them. But there is one thing that can never be taken from Paul and Silas, and that is God's love. There's not a weapon in this world that can separate you from the life and love of Jesus. Nothing can separate you from God's love and therefore you can always be joyful because you'll always have Him.

If you get your joy from your footy team winning, that can be taken away from you. If you get your joy from the house you own, the position you hold, those things can be taken from you. But if Jesus is the source of your

Jail House Rock

joy, then you will have it forever because you will have him forever. Paul and Silas are locked up, but they're actually completely free. Completely free from fear, and completely free from uncertainty. They don't know what the future holds but they know the goodness of the One who holds the future.

Paul and Silas continue to belt out their tunes when the most dramatic thing happens—an earthquake strikes. It's not clear whether the ground only moves inside the prison or if it is felt further afield, but all the doors fly open, and the chains fall off every prisoner. This is good news for the prisoners, but very bad news for the jailer. If a prisoner escapes, it's the jailer who suffers the consequences; he'll likely be put to death for this. The jailer fears the worst and draws his sword to kill himself.

Paul shouts, "Stop! Don't kill yourself! We are all here!"[105]

The jailer falls before Paul and Silas trembling, asking, "Sirs, what must I do to be saved?"[106]

That night the jailer and his entire family come to know Jesus. What a night!

Paul and Silas chose to worship God and praise him for His goodness even though they were having the worst of days. It takes courage to remember that God's goodness is bigger than our daily experience. Our circumstances are not always good, but Paul and Silas remember that God is always good even in the midst of pain and trouble. Paul and Silas are brave, they find joy in every circumstance

---
105 Acts 16:28
106 Acts 16:30

because their joy is found in Jesus.

Elvis had a complex faith; he sang beautiful gospel songs and was raised in the church. He also lived a very worldly lifestyle and had a massive drug addiction.

One time Elvis talked about performing saying, "We do two shows a night for five weeks. A lotta times we'll go upstairs and sing until daylight—gospel songs. We grew up with it... It more or less puts your mind at ease. It does mine."[107]

It seems Elvis also found that praising God at midnight is a good way to re-orientate your mind away from your troubling circumstances and back onto God's unending love.

It takes courage to praise God in prison; it takes courage to thank Him in troubling circumstances. The brave remember that there are no circumstances where God isn't present, where God's love doesn't reach. Corrie Ten Boom, who spent time in a German concentration camp during World War Two, once said: "There is no pit so deep, that God's love isn't deeper still." The brave know Jesus is with them in everything and so find joy in every situation.

Bible Story: Acts 16

Press Pause: *Where can I find joy in my situation?*

Verse to remember:
 Always be joyful. Never stop praying. Be thankful in all

[107] https://www.graceland.com/quotes-by-elvis

circumstances, for this is God's will for you who belong to Christ Jesus. (1 Thessalonians 5:16-18)

18.

Prison Break

Brave is forgiving

Botham Jean, a 26-year-old accountant, was shot dead in his apartment by policewoman Amber Guyger. Jean and Guyger lived in the same apartment building, with Jean living on the fourth floor directly above Guyger. One night returning home from work after a long shift, Guyger claimed she confused Botham's apartment with her own and that she had walked in to find a dangerous intruder. This is hard to believe given that Jean was sitting in his apartment eating ice cream. But, even if Jean had been an ice cream bandit, shooting him dead looks like an overreaction.

This case caused outrage throughout America because it was yet another case of a white police officer killing an unarmed African American. When Guyger was initially charged with the lesser offence of manslaughter, many saw it as an example of racial bias. People took to the streets in protest, and Guyger's charges were later upgraded to murder. She was found guilty and sentenced to ten years in prison.

Something remarkable happened during Guyger's trial when Brandt Jean took the stand to give a victim impact statement.

The eighteen-year-old younger brother of Botham Jean turned to Guyger and said, "I don't want to say twice or for the hundredth time how much you've taken from us, I think you know that...I forgive you and if you go to God and ask Him, He will forgive you. I love you just like anyone else and I'm not going to say I hope you rot and die like my brother did...I don't even want you to go to jail, I want the best for you. I love you as a person and I don't wish anything bad on you."

With the court in stunned silence, Brandt made a radical request, "I don't know if this is possible, but can I give her a hug?" Six long seconds passed before the judge gave her approval. Brandt Jean embraced his brother's killer, and Guyger was overcome with emotion, sobbing uncontrollably.

How in the world did Brandt Jean find it within himself to forgive someone who had hurt him so badly?

Later Brandt would explain his decision saying, "If you are trying to forgive her remember that's she's a human being. She still deserves love; she made a mistake that she probably truly regrets. If you want to forgive her understand that God forgave you."[108]

---

[108] https://abcnews.go.com/GMA/News/botham-jeans-brother-discusses-emotional-courtroom-hug-amber/story?id=66055688

Prison Break

Brandt could have so easily held onto anger, and while Guyger was in jail, Brandt could have been in a prison of his own bitterness.

Nearly all of us have people in our lives that we're not happy with, people who have hurt us either intentionally or unintentionally. Some of our relationships are broken due to hurt and offence. Being unable to forgive isn't a problem solely for unbelievers, followers of Jesus often find forgiveness a big challenge too.

Saul meets Christ in dramatic circumstances when Jesus appears to him on the Road to Damascus.

To set the scene:
Saul is transformed from jailing Christians to joining them! Renamed Paul, he writes many of the letters in the New Testament, and in his letter to the Church in Philippi, we find Paul offering some clear instructions:

> Now I appeal to Euodia and Syntyche. Please, because you belong to the Lord, settle your disagreement.[109]

We don't know many details about these two women. We know they are part of the Philippi Church. They worked with Paul to share the good news of Jesus. We know they had a falling out. Whatever the cause of their disagreement, whether it was big or trivial, isn't important. Paul says that these women belong to the Lord. They are followers of Jesus and yet there's been a dispute that needs settling. Paul encourages these women by telling them that because they belong to the Lord, they need to

---
[109] Philippians 4:2

resolve this matter. Christ has forgiven them so, regardless of whose fault it is, they should be able to forgive each other. Paul has experience with conflict between believers; one time he had a falling out with Barnabas.

When Paul becomes a Christian, the other believers are terrified of him. He has locked up many Christians and had some put to death, so their hesitation about trusting him is understandable. It is Barnabas who takes a risk by meeting with Paul and speaking up for him. He tells the believers that Paul's conversion is genuine. Later Barnabas is asked to pastor a church in Antioch. Barnabas brings Paul to the Church and together they teach the Church at Antioch to follow Jesus. During a time of worship, the Lord speaks to the leaders in Antioch telling them to send Barnabas and Paul out as missionaries. Barnabas and Paul set out to proclaim the good news of Jesus and start new churches, and John-Mark, a cousin of Barnabas, comes along as their helper.

Barnabas and Paul hit the road travelling to Cyprus, Pamphylia, Iconium, Lystra, and Derbe, spreading the gospel and dodging death at every turn. What an adventure! What a partnership! John-Mark doesn't have a great trip though, and while they are in Pamphylia, he leaves Barnabas and Paul and goes home. Sometime later Paul wants to go on a second missionary journey to visit the believers and churches in all the cities they visited and see how they are going. Barnabas agrees and wants to bring John-Mark along, but Paul thinks that's a bad idea because he quit on the last mission. These are no tourist trips, Paul was almost stoned to death on the first missionary journey, and they are not for the faint of heart.

Prison Break

Barnabas wants to give his cousin a second chance. As Barnabas gave Paul a chance when no one believed in him, is it too much to ask Paul to give John-Mark a second opportunity?

Who's right and who's wrong? Is Paul right to think about the importance of the mission, and not having a quitter on the team? Is Barnabas right to give John-Mark another chance? Is Barnabas' family allegiance to John-Mark clouding his judgment? Is Paul being too stubborn? Whoever is actually right, Paul and Barnabas feel so strongly about it they split up. Paul chooses Silas and goes to Syria, Barnabas takes John-Mark and goes to Cyrus. Did it have to come to this? Couldn't these two Christian leaders have found a way to resolve their differences? Couldn't someone have compromised? I think these two great leaders let themselves down. They weren't arguing over important Christian beliefs, they were arguing about how to run a mission trip. They let the little things ruin the big picture.

There is, however, a twist to come in this disappointing episode. We discover many years later that Paul and John-Mark have reunited. About ten years after the ugly dispute, Paul writes in one of his letters:

> Aristarchus, who is in prison with me, sends you his greetings, and so does Mark, Barnabas's cousin. As you were instructed before, make Mark welcome if he comes your way.[110]

And towards the very end of Paul's life in one of his final letters he writes:

---
[110] Colossians 4:10

> Luke alone is with me. Get Mark and bring him with you, for he is very useful to me for ministry.[111]

News Flash! Paul, who didn't even want John-Mark to go on a mission trip with him, now thinks John-Mark is useful! More than just useful—John-Mark is known today as the author of the Gospel of Mark. What a change of heart from Paul. I wonder what it would have been like when John-Mark and Paul reconnected for the first time. Did John-Mark say sorry for quitting? Did Paul say sorry for being stubborn? Whatever was said, Paul and John-Mark were able to forgive because they had both been forgiven by God. They were able to put aside the past, renew their relationship, and work together in spreading the good news of Jesus. And, because Paul was able to reconcile with John-Mark, he is able to encourage Euodia and Syntyche to do the same.

No one's pretending that forgiveness is easy, it's a challenging journey. If we believe forgiveness is important, we need to practice it ourselves. If we appreciate how God forgave us for all the sins we committed against Him then we must pass that forgiveness to those who have sinned against us. This means Euodia should forgive Syntyche even if Syntyche won't forgive Euodia. We can't control what others will do, we can't make others be sorry, we can't make others talk to us. What we can do is take the same brave step that Brandt Jean took and forgive.

It's said that refusing to forgive is like drinking poison and expecting the other person to die. Unforgiveness is doing far more damage to you than it is to anyone else.

---

[111] 2 Timothy 4:11

Prison Break

Lewis Smedes puts it well when he says, *To forgive is to set a prisoner free and discover that the prisoner was you.*

It's time to make a prison break.

Bible Story: Acts 15:36-41

Press Pause: *Who do I need to forgive?*

Verse to remember:
> Make allowance for each other's faults and forgive anyone who offends you. Remember, the Lord forgave you, so you must forgive others. (Colossians 3:13)

19.

Making a Splash

Brave is passing the message on

Chris Christie was an American politician. He was a straight-shooting, politically incorrect, 'tell it like it is' politician who took no prisoners and didn't mind a bit of the limelight. He served as Governor of the State of New Jersey, and once unsuccessfully ran for US President. And, on August 13th, 2014, Chris Christie participated in the Ice Bucket Challenge.

The Ice Bucket Challenge was a fundraising and awareness campaign for Motor Neuron Disease. Participants were nominated to do the Ice Bucket Challenge by their friends. First, they would pour ice and cold water into a bucket and make a video. Then, they would nominate three other people to take on the challenge before tipping the bucket of freezing cold water over their heads. Participants usually made a financial donation to MND research.

When Chris Christie did the Ice Bucket Challenge he nominated Facebook CEO, Mark Zuckerberg. The next day

Mark Zuckerberg participated in the Ice Bucket Challenge and, not surprisingly, uploaded his video to Facebook. Zuckerberg had nominated Bill Gates, the founder of the Microsoft company, who is one of the world's richest men—so he could afford to build a mechanical device to tip the bucket over his head. When it was his turn, Gates nominated American television host Ryan Seacrest, who in turn nominated David Beckham, a former English soccer superstar. David Beckham nominated movie star Leonardo DiCaprio, who nominated Stephen Harper, the Prime Minister of Canada at time. Despite Harper declining to participate, the challenge continued to spread all over the world with over 17 million Ice Bucket Challenge videos posted online.

The Ice Bucket Challenge worked because it was simple and almost anyone could participate. If you were rich like Bill Gates, you could build an ice bucket device, but all that was really needed was a bucket and water. The challenge was personal, people nominated and were nominated by their friends. The ice bucket challenge may have been uncomfortable, but it was for a good cause.

Jesus uses the same method to spread His message across the world.

To set the scene:

He starts with a small number of followers. It's well known that Jesus has 12 disciples, and at one point He sends out 72 followers[112] and, after His resurrection, He appears to more than 500[113]. These are relatively small numbers. How did this small bunch of people spread the message

---

[112] Luke 10:1
[113] 1 Corinthians 15:6

of Jesus in such a way that 2000 years later more than 2 billion people would call Jesus king?

Consider another example: The best-selling book of all time. *The Twilight Saga* novels have sold more than 100 million copies, *The Lord of the Rings* novels have sold over 150 million copies, and the *Harry Potter* series sold an impressive 500 million books. But the Bible is in a league of its own with over five billion copies printed. Christmas and Easter are two of the most significant holidays in the Western World, representing the bookends of Jesus' life with Christmas marking His birth and Easter His death and resurrection. They are celebrated in every corner of the Earth, how did the good news of Jesus become so widespread?

Philip is a leader in the early Church. As the Church rapidly grows, the apostles realise the Church require more leaders, and Philip is one of the seven chosen. Jesus had commanded his followers to spread the good news of Jesus everywhere; to Jerusalem (their city), Judea (their country), Samaria (other nations), and the ends of the earth (everywhere else). So far, the Church exists only in Jerusalem but that is all about to change.

Stephen, another of the seven chosen leaders is arrested. Stephen is described as a man full of God's grace and power. Many Jews try to argue with him, but they are no match for Stephen's wisdom. These Jews resort to lying about Stephen to have him arrested. The very same tactics were used against Jesus. When it comes time for Stephen to speak, he recounts Israel's entire history from Abraham, Moses, and King David. The Jewish leaders don't care to listen and before he is finished, they stone him to death. A great wave of persecution breaks out against Christians in Jerusalem. The violence is led by Saul, a Jewish religious leader who embarks on a campaign of terror designed to destroy the Church. Saul goes on a rampage, killing every follower of Jesus he can. Philip escapes Jerusalem as believers flee for their lives.

Philip escapes to the city of Samaria. The Samaritans are notoriously hostile towards the Jews. Yet Jesus had told His followers to proclaim the good news in Samaria and so Phillip proclaims Jesus to them. Many Samaritans start believing that Jesus is the saviour of the world. Philip is making a splash proclaiming Jesus wherever he goes. Before Saul's campaign of terror, the Church was located solely in Jerusalem. Thanks to his persecution, the Church is now in multiple locations and includes multiple cultures. Jews and Samaritans are now brothers and sisters in God's family.

You would think God would want Philip to stay in Samaria for a long time and keep building the Church, but God has a new mission for Phillip. An angel tells Philip to go south. With those general instructions, Philip sets off and happens to meet the treasurer of Ethiopia. Philip walks along near the treasurer's chariot. Philip hears him reading from the book of Isaiah, one of the books in the Old Testament.

Philip asks, "Do you understand what you are reading?"[114]

The treasurer invites Philip to explain it to him. Philip

---

[114] Acts 8:30

explains the passage in Isaiah and the whole message about Jesus. As they travel, they come to some water, and they stop the chariot. The treasurer announces that he wants to be baptized as a follower of Jesus—Phillip is making a splash. God's family now includes Jews, Samaritans...and Ethiopians. As Philip baptizes Ethiopia's treasurer, God takes Philip away. While the treasurer has lost Philip, he rejoices because he now shares Philip's faith in Jesus. The treasurer continues on his journey to take the good news of Jesus to Africa, the gospel just keeps spreading.

Philip's preaching impacts great crowds of Samaritans but only one Ethiopian. But if that Ethiopian passes the message onto someone else who passes it on again, it won't be long before the good news is heard everywhere. The treasurer was the very first Ethiopian believer but today Christianity is the most common religion in Ethiopia. Never underestimate what God can do as you share the good news with just one person.

Philip ran for his life from Jerusalem as any of us might do. Philip was brave in that wherever he found himself he declared the good news of Jesus. We too can be brave and share the hope of Jesus wherever we find ourselves. Like the Ice Bucket Challenge, sharing the message of Jesus is simple and personal. It involves us sharing our story with those we come across. As Philip can attest, sharing Jesus can sometimes be uncomfortable but it's for an eternally good cause.

We don't hear much about Philip after God takes him away. He preaches God's good news everywhere he goes until he settles in Caesarea. Many years later Philip has an unexpected guest at his home, the apostle Paul. Paul was previously known as the murderous Saul, that religious leader who had Phillip's friend Stephen put to death. Saul was the reason Philip had to flee Jerusalem. Saul himself found Jesus in a dramatic encounter not long after Stephen's death. Instead of fighting against the followers of Jesus, he joined them. Paul will spend the rest of his life following Philip's example in making a splash by passing on the message of Jesus.

In a strange irony, Paul spends the night at Philip's house, something unimaginable years earlier. Philip no longer needs to fear Paul, they are now brothers in the same family, a family which includes Jews, Samaritans, Ethiopians, and a growing list of nations. By this time Philip has four daughters who have the gift of prophecy.[115]

At every opportunity, Philip passes on the message. He passes on the message while serving as a church leader in Jerusalem, he preaches the good news when he escapes to Samaria, he explains the message of Jesus to the treasurer of Ethiopia, and he shares the good news with his own children. His daughters have come to know the saving message of Jesus and are serving Jesus like their dad. One of Philip's daughters was Hermione of Ephesus who, like dad, makes a splash by sharing the good news of Jesus wherever she goes. Those she led to faith passed on the message to others who passed it onto others who have now passed it onto us. Who will you pass the message onto? Will you make a splash with the good news?

---

[115] Acts 21:9

Making a Splash

Bible story: Acts chapter 8

Press Pause: *Who will you pass the message onto?*

Verse to remember:
But the believers who were scattered preached the Good News about Jesus wherever they went. (Acts 8:4)

20.

Dive for the Line

Brave never quits

Vontae Davis was a quarterback playing for the New York-based Buffalo Bills. Davis was a talented player, making the all-star pro-ball team on two occasions, but he will always be remembered for the way he retired. Things weren't going well for the Buffalo Bills as the halftime siren sounded, they were trailing the Los Angeles Chargers 28-6.

While their coach was trying to regroup for the second half, Davis had other ideas—he decided to retire.

The ten-year veteran of the game said, "I shouldn't be out there anymore." Davis got changed, left the stadium, and went home while his teammates were out on the field fighting hard to bring the score back to a more respectable 31-20 defeat.

Could there be a more disrespectful way to retire than to walk out on your team at halftime? In contrast, consider rugby league's Cooper Cronk. He played most of his career for the Melbourne Storm but in the twilight of his career switched to play for the Sydney Roosters. In his first season with the Roosters, Cronk found himself in the Grand Final against his former side. Just twelve months earlier Cronk had held the premiership aloft with his Storm teammates. Now he was lining up against them and, to make matters worse; his shoulder was broken.

The previous week Cronk had injured his shoulder in the preliminary final. In the media, it was portrayed as a race against time for Cronk to be fit for the Grand Final. The reality was Cronk had a 15cm fracture through his scapula. Everyone came to the same conclusion: there's no way he can play. Cronk spent the week having painkilling injections, CT scans, and ultrasounds.

As he tossed up whether to play or not to play, his wife told him, "What are you carrying on about, you've been given the chance to play in a Grand Final, suck it up." Cronk played and led his team to victory.

Vontae Davis threw in the towel while Cooper Cronk played with a broken shoulder. How can we find the courage to press on despite the setbacks and difficulties we're facing? How can we find the courage to never quit? Someone in the Bible who never quit is Paul. Once known as Saul, he arrested and violently persecuted Christians.

To set the scene:
He is on his way to the city of Damascus to wage war on believers. As he approaches the city, light from heaven flashes around him and he falls to the ground.

Dive for the Line

Saul hears a voice, "Saul, Saul, why are you persecuting me?"[116] Saul is dumbfounded.

"Who are you Lord?"[117] Saul asks.

The reply could not have been clearer, "I am Jesus, whom you are persecuting."[118]

Jesus takes it personally when His people are attacked. Saul is blinded until he is prayed for and healed. Suddenly Saul who was in Damascus to arrest believers now believes! Saul starts preaching in the synagogue that Jesus is the saviour of the world!

The local Jews are outraged. Just as Saul planned to kill Christians, now the Jews are planning to kill him. Saul proudly entered Damascus breathing murderous threats against the followers of Jesus. He leaves the city under the cover of darkness, lowered over the city wall in a basket.

The trouble didn't end there. Saul is renamed Paul and he takes the good news of Jesus on several mission trips. Many lives are changed through Paul's trips but there's plenty of trouble. He is jailed in Philippi, there are riots in Ephesus, and he is nearly stoned to death in Lystra. Paul once described his troubles this way:

> Five different times the Jewish leaders gave me thirty-nine lashes. Three times I was beaten with rods. Once I was stoned. Three times I was shipwrecked. Once I spent a whole night and a day adrift at sea. I have travelled on many long journeys. I have faced danger from rivers and

---
116 Acts 9:4
117 Acts 9:5
118 Acts 9:5

from robbers. I have faced danger from my own people, the Jews, as well as from the Gentiles. I have faced danger in the cities, in the deserts, and on the seas. And I have faced danger from men who claim to be believers but are not. I have worked hard and long, enduring many sleepless nights. I have been hungry and thirsty and have often gone without food. I have shivered in the cold, without enough clothing to keep me warm.[119]

Following, Jesus had changed Paul's life, but it didn't free him of problems. Despite his sufferings, Paul carries on but some of his friends quit. Demas doesn't get much publicity in the Bible, but he is mentioned three times. In the books of Philemon and Colossians, Demas is listed as one of Paul's co-workers. Some years later Paul says:

> Demas has deserted me because he loves the things of this life and has gone to Thessalonica.[120]

We don't know much about Demas. We know he travelled with Paul proclaiming the good news. We know he quit the team and he did so because he loved the things of this life. Demas wanted a comfortable life; he didn't want to suffer the beatings and the jailing's that Paul constantly faced. Like Vontae Davis, he quit at half time. Paul, who suffered much pain, is like Cooper Cronk playing the final with a broken shoulder. There are two reasons Paul was able to bravely endure despite the sufferings he faced.

Paul had God's love which could never be taken away from him. Secondly, Paul could endure such hard trials because he had his eyes on eternity. When Cooper Cronk was playing in a Grand Final, he knew he only had to play

---

[119] 2 Corinthians 11:24
[120] 2 Timothy 4:10

Dive for the Line

for 80 minutes and enjoy the victory for years to come. Cronk had a reason for embracing suffering and so did Paul. Here's how Paul described his focus:

> I don't mean to say that I have already achieved these things or that I have already reached perfection. But I press on to possess that perfection for which Christ Jesus first possessed me. No, dear brothers and sisters, I have not achieved it, but I focus on this one thing: Forgetting the past and looking forward to what lies ahead, I press on to reach the end of the race and receive the heavenly prize for which God, through Christ Jesus, is calling us.[121]

Paul wasn't focused on the here and now, he was focused on forever. This life on earth is short, it's here today, and gone tomorrow. In fifty years, the things that worry you today will probably be long forgotten. Ten thousand years from now, how significant will your current worries be? Paul was able to sing in jail because he knew eternity was on the way. Another time Paul was in jail he didn't know whether he would be released or be executed. Either way, Paul didn't mind saying:

> For to me, living means living for Christ, and dying is even better. But if I live, I can do more fruitful work for Christ. So, I really don't know which is better. I'm torn between two desires: I long to go and be with Christ, which would be far better for me. But for your sakes, it is better that I continue to live.[122]

Paul can't lose. If Paul lives, he can continue to share the good news of Jesus but if he dies it's even better. That's why Paul could rejoice in the middle of suffering. Paul

---
[121] Philippians 3:12-14
[122] Philippians 1:21

knew nobody could take away God's love, and he had his eyes focused on forever.

Dive for the line
Shaunae Miller-Ubio was an Olympic athlete from the Bahamas. At the 2016 games, Miller was in the final of the 400 meters. Miller was up against Allyson Felix, the current world champion and six-time Olympic Gold medallist. Miller ran the race of her life, heading into the final straight in the lead with Felix closing fast. As they approached the finish line it looked like Felix would catch Miller, then the unthinkable happened: Miller dived for the line. Some commentators described Miller as collapsing across the line, others remarked she might win a medal for Olympic diving. Miller ran faster than she had ever run before and her dive for the line won her Olympic Gold. She gave it everything she had.

Paul wasn't always a Christian but after meeting Jesus he spent the rest of his life proclaiming the good news despite the suffering that came. He gave it everything. Some of Paul's last words were:

> The time of my death is near. I have fought the good fight, I have finished the race, and I have remained faithful. And now the prize awaits me.[123]

May we be brave like Paul and proclaim the good news of Christ until the very end. Let's give it everything we have and dive for the line.

---

[123] 2 Timothy 4:6-8

Dive for the Line

Bible Story: Acts chapter 9, Philippians chapter 3 and 2 Timothy chapter 4.

Press Pause: *Am I tempted to quit when the going gets tough?*

Verse to remember:
So, let's not get tired of doing what is good. At just the right time we will reap a harvest of blessing if we don't give up. (Galatians 6:9)

About the Author

Travis Barnes works at Creek Street Christian College as a teacher and chaplain. He has spent his adult life pointing the next generation towards Jesus at schools, churches, beach missions and camps.

Travis is passionate about presenting the hope of Jesus in a clear and engaging way. He hopes to see the next generation of young people become fearless followers of Jesus who live bravely for His eternal cause.

Travis lives in Central Victoria with his wife Cara and two daughters.

Are you Brave in Making?
Connect online and find more Brave resources at
www.bravetoday.net

www.ingramcontent.com/pod-product-compliance
Lightning Source LLC
Chambersburg PA
CBHW050314010526
44107CB00055B/2238